Weathering Storms:
Human Resources in Difficult Times

Weathering Storms:
Human Resources in Difficult Times

Society for Human Resource Management | Alexandria, Virginia | USA
www.shrm.org | © 2008

This book is published by the Society for Human Resource Management (SHRM®). The interpretations, conclusions, and recommendations in this book are those of the authors and do not necessarily represent those of the publishers.

The Society for Human Resource Management (SHRM) is the world's largest professional association devoted to human resource management. Our mission is to serve the needs of HR professionals by providing the most current and comprehensive resources, and to advance the profession by promoting HR's essential, strategic role. Founded in 1948, SHRM represents members in over 140 countries, and has a network of more than 575 affiliated chapters in the United States, as well as offices in China and India. Visit SHRM at www.shrm.org.

Interior and Cover Design: James McGinnis, Kellyn Lombardi

Library of Congress Cataloging-in-Publication Data

Weathering storms: human resources in difficult times.
     p. cm.
  Includes index.
  ISBN 978-1-58644-134-0
1. Personnel management. I. Society for Human Resource Management (U.S.)
HF5549.W4114 2008
658.3--dc22
                                    2008045835
Printed in the United States of America.
10 9 8 7 6 5 4 3 2 1

08-0637

Contents

Introduction: Making the Right Decisions During Economic Downturns (Peter Cappelli) 1

Part I: Proactive HR Solutions

1. When Business Hiccups—The Prepared HR Pro (John Sweeney).................... 8
2. Managing Employees in a Downsized Environment (Marcia Scott, MD) 10
3. Managing a Downturn (Susan J. Wells)..14
4. Riding Out the Storm with Clear Explanations (Steve Taylor) 20
5. Many Plan To Scale Back Benefits, Pay Raises as Economy Slows (Stephen Miller) 24
6. As Staffing Slips, Recruiters Must Work Harder (Theresa Minton-Eversole)... 26
7. Recruiting Grads (Theresa Minton-Eversole)....................................... 30
8. Address Financial Ills To Reduce Other Workplace Problems (Rebecca R. Hastings, SPHR) 34
9. Prune Employees Carefully (Adrienne Fox)....................................... 38
10. Reduction in Force and Employees with Performance Problems................... 44
11. Employers Using Benefits To Help Employees Fill the Tank............................ 46
12. Tighter Times, Leaner Technology (Jennifer Taylor Arnold) 48
13. Soft Real Estate Market Impacts Corporate Relocation Programs (Stephen Miller) 54
14. Personalized Transition: Workers Are Demanding More Sophisticated Outplacement Services (Donna M. Owens)....................................... 56
15. Easing the Burden of Financial Stress in the Workplace (Elizabeth Agnvall)... 62
16. Easing the Burden of Employees' Debt (Peter Weaver and Gina Rollins)........ 66
17. Employee Forgivable Loans (Anne St. Martin)................................. 72
18. Keep Workers 401(k)-Focused (Nancy Hatch Woodward)................................74
19. The Difference between a Furlough, a Layoff, and a Reduction in Force........ 80
20. Selecting Employees for Layoff.. 84

Part II: The Tools: Definitions, Guidelines, Sample Policies, Letters, and Forms

21. WARN Notice 90

22. Older Workers Act Waiver.. 92

23. Letter of Transfer... 94

24. Transportation Benefit Plan Enrollment/Change/Cancellation Form.............. 96

25. Transportation Benefit Plan Reimbursement Request 98

26. Telecommuting Application 100

27. Compressed Workweek 102

28. Flextime Request Form.. 106

29. Flexible Work Arrangement Agreement 108

30. Alternative Work Schedule Policy.. 110

31. Job-Sharing Memo of Understanding.. 112

32. Summer Flextime Policy 114

33. Summer Flextime Request Form.. 116

34. Take the Summer Off Program Policy 118

35. Work Sabbatical Policy.. 120

36. Work Sabbatical Leave Form... 124

37. Voluntary Reduction in Force (RIF) Separation Program 126

38. 401(k) Plan: Hardship Withdrawal Request.. 130

39. Layoff and Recall Policy 134

40. Low-Need Time.. 136

41. Separation Agreement and Release of Claims 138

42. Reduction in Force Selection and Severance Pay.. 142

43. Involuntary Termination Policy... 146

44. Sample Letter: Benefits Changes Due to Reduction in Hours 148

45. Sample Letter: Layoff or RIF—Lack of Work.. 150

46. Sample Letter: Reduction in Force—Declining Sales.................................... 152

47. Sample Letter: Termination Because of Layoff, Downsizing, Etc.................. 154

Conclusion: After the Layoff: How Are You Feeling? (Adrienne Fox).................. 156

Additional Resources 164

About the Contributors 168

Endnotes 170

Index...172

Introduction

Making the Right Decisions During Economic Downturns

Peter Cappelli

Layoffs represent a relatively new challenge for the human resource function. The option of laying off workers raises fundamental, strategic questions such as when to do them, how to carry them out, and even whether to do them at all.

The notion of layoffs, at least the way we think of them now, is a relatively new phenomenon. Layoffs represent the involuntary termination of employees for reasons other than the performance of the employees. Through the 1970s, companies laid off workers only as a last resort, and then only production workers (almost never white-collar employees), typically only when the recessions associated with business cycles forced demand for products sharply down. Even in those circumstances, layoffs were temporary: Employees could expect to be rehired when demand picked back up. These arrangements were formalized in unionized operations with supplemental unemployment benefit programs, whereby the employer continued to pay laid-off workers some proportion of their previous wages for up to years at a time to keep them from moving on to jobs elsewhere. The unions that created these programs did so explicitly with the goal of reducing the incentives for employers to lay off workers. The fact that layoffs were a temporary phenomenon is demonstrated by the fact that the U.S. Bureau of Labor Statistics did not even track permanent job losses until the mid-1980s with the new term "displaced workers."

Layoffs as we now know them represent something quite different. First, layoffs are virtually always permanent job losses. Laid-off workers rarely ever expect to be called back. Second, layoffs now affect all employees, not just production workers. Indeed, in the 1980s, managerial employees were actually more likely to be laid off than their colleagues in other positions. Third, while recessions remain an important cause, layoffs are increasingly driven now by internal factors, such as restructuring programs, changes in business strategy, and a press for increased operating efficiency.

This contemporary version of layoffs got going in 1981 as part of the worst recession since the Great Depression. The layoffs began because of the recession-related downturn in demand, but companies then began to restructure operations in ways that reduced the need for labor permanently. As a result, the laid-off workers were not rehired. And these restructuring efforts, what became known as "reengineering," soon spread to white collar and managerial areas, leading to layoffs there as well. Even as the economy improved, layoffs continued, and the causes of layoffs began to shift, with fewer being attributed to the overall economy and more associated with efforts to improve productivity.

Layoffs have become so common that we more or less take them for granted now. But it is worth asking the basic question, why do we have layoffs at all? Several factors stand out. The first and most obvious issue is the pressure to cut costs, which increased in recent decades as firms have come under more pressure from investors to increase profits. In fact, companies announce more layoffs than they actually carry out, apparently in the belief that the investor community thinks that layoffs are a good thing. Labor is far and away the biggest share of operating expenses, and if employers cannot use employees for some reason, it is very expensive to keep carrying them. This helps explain why employers have begun to layoff workers sooner in economic downturns. The drawback to laying off workers, of course, is that the employer is cutting assets that have been important to the company. If we argue by analogy and think of employees as the equivalent of something like machine tools, it would seem risky for a business that wants to keep operating to sell off its machinery when business turned down. What will we do when business picks up?

That leads us to a second important factor increasing the incidence of layoffs, and that is the dramatically improved ability to hire employees on a just-in-time basis. When business picks back up, employers have found it remarkably easy to go back into the labor market and hire new workers – across all occupations and skills – who can expand their operations. What happens when business picks up following a layoff is simply that employers go back into the labor market, hire a new crop of workers, and start again. The cost of letting workers go is therefore greatly reduced.

Another reason why the costs of letting workers go is reduced is because companies change their business strategies so frequently now, and in the process change the organizational competencies they need to pursue new strategies. A company that decides to abandon one market and move into another, for example, may feel that it no longer needs the competencies aimed at the old market, some of which are embedded in the knowledge, skills, and abilities of current employees. Because those competencies are redundant, continuing to pay for them represents a serious drain on the organization, and that creates the pressure to layoff. At the same time, the organization may need new competencies in order to move into new markets or to position itself in different ways. Therefore many companies find themselves laying off and then hiring again as a way to switch competencies.

Finally, the costs of laying off workers have decreased as more companies did it. The reputational costs of cutting workers, in many cases breaking what had been implicit lifetime employment arrangements, declined for firms as the more firms engaged in layoffs, and they became more acceptable.

The basic question for employers is whether they should pursue a strategy of layoffs at all. Human resources needs to be at the center of that discussion. In many companies, the decision to layoff workers is made elsewhere, by the financial and accounting staff, in part based on the assumption that layoffs will improve the financial situation of the company. The research on layoffs, however, has been fairly consistent in finding that the financial performance of companies does not improve following layoffs. One spurious reason why that might be so is simply because companies that layoff are often already in trouble, and even if layoffs were the right tactic, they may not be enough to solve the problems that led to them in the first place. But these results are not encouraging for those who engage in them.

Part of the value that HR brings to those decisions is expert knowledge about the costs of layoffs. One important aspect of those costs is the difficulty in rebuilding the organization's human capital in the future. Yes, layoffs save money, but will we be able to hire the skills we need in the future if we let the employees go at this point? If so, how long will it take, and how much will it cost? Other costs of layoffs include the effects on morale of the existing workforce and effects on the ability to hire in the future when employers lay off.

Another part of the expert knowledge that HR can bring to the question of layoffs is a consideration of the workforce alternatives to them. Depending what the challenge is that layoffs are designed to solve, employers need to consider a range of approaches in order to understand if any might be preferable. If the problem is a temporary downturn in business, for example, reduced hours or short-term furloughs may allow the employer to keep the workforce together when business returns; if the issue is the need to change competencies, retraining the existing workforce might be an option worth considering. None of this should suggest that the answer is to never layoff. It is a judgment call that can only be made correctly if all these factors are considered.

A second fundamental question concerning layoffs is, if we do them, how should they be carried out? Another explanation for the poor record that layoffs have in terms of subsequent performance could be that the way layoffs are often conducted often creates lots of new problems. One of the most important conclusions from research about the complications from layoffs is that they often have extremely deleterious effects on those who survive the job cuts as they can experience guilt and freeze up in terms of subsequent performance or believe that their survival was simply luck and become preoccupied with finding another job before the next round of layoffs.

A great deal of substantive knowledge is required to conduct layoffs well. Among the issues that we know reduce the risks of bad outcomes are developing a plan, and communicating it to employees, indicating both why the layoffs and necessary and how the operations will improve following the layoffs; as part of that plan, being able to explain to those who survived layoffs why they made it, that the process wasn't random, and presumably why they are important for the new vision of the organization going forward; finding ways to treat the employees who are laid off with dignity and respect, not only because it is the right thing to do but also because it affects the reputation of the organization with its own employees and with future hires.

The articles in this volume can help arm us with the knowledge necessary to make the right decisions concerning layoffs.

Should you lay off – how hard is it to start up again?

(Cut dead wood)

Alternatives to layoffs that might achieve similar results.

When to do it, what's the effect?

How to do it.

Proactive HR Solutions

1 When Business Hiccups— The Prepared HR Pro

John Sweeney

The news is dismal—falling home prices amid record foreclosures, the disappearance of credit, inflation-eroding pay, the declining value of the dollar on the world stage, and impending layoffs—a continuing downward spiral, which means that it is time for HR to get busy! So, regardless of whether or not your business has been affected thus far, HR professionals should begin looking at measures that they can bring forward to help ensure the health of the business and its staff during downturns.

Major shifts in economic conditions always should alert HR pros that circumstances have changed and that they play a lead strategic role in minimizing a company's risks during periods of economic turbulence. Thus, HR needs to step up to look at the impact of business disruptions and lay out action plans and alternatives for review with the senior management team. The following checklist will serve as a baseline for being prepared to discuss changing business climate issues with senior management.

- Review plans for implementation of a new program, initiative, or expansion of business to determine whether the timing is on target or whether to defer action.
- Participate in cross-discipline reviews of all business practices to evaluate internal business processes in the event of neutral or declining revenue periods.
- Review recruitment practices to determine if recruitment efforts should be suspended, retargeted, or frozen.

- Take a look forward at your contingent hiring practices—need for independent contractors, temporary employees, and/or interns/summer help—and revisit planned quarterly hiring forecasts.
- Meet with senior management to determine current staffing vs. budget, discuss reductions in overtime and/or staff, and staff scheduling changes and/or reductions.
- Review planned wage/salary or incentive compensation plans to see whether they should remain as planned, retargeted, or frozen.
- Review possible changes to training and development budgets and associated travel costs.
- For outsourced services/providers, review contractual obligations to evaluate whether these should be continued, amended, or terminated.
- Review current workforce practices. If business conditions are forecasted to deteriorate, consider reduction or elimination of business travel expenses, job-sharing to retain talent, scheduled hour reductions, telecommuting to reduce facility costs, or suspension of special pay arrangements that are not legally mandated.
- Concurrently, plan how HR can best offer free community or other low-cost resources or company-provided initiatives that can be brought to bear to help current staff weather their own financial issues.

2 Managing Employees in a Downsized Environment

Marcia Scott, MD

While downsizing may be a corporate vision of change for the employer, it's a vision of job loss for employees. This scenario creates a daunting task for the HR professional who must help separated employees find work, money, and a new future. At the same time, HR must help retained employees confront new challenges.

In the view of an employee, a downsizing causes many losses—diminished security, increased work, changed priorities, and disruptions in relationships, to name a few. Specifically, the organization must cope with the loss of leaders who once defined the organization's character. Also lost are long-term support staff who hold knowledge about the organization's operations and its history.

There will be many questions. Am I safe? Do I have to prove myself again? What's in this for me? HR has a major role in dealing with its effects on individual productivity and on the organizational process.

Assessing Your Company

Human and organizational responses to change are very fluid. Individuals may not react characteristically, depending on the nature of the organization and how the change began. However, there are many opportunities to evaluate the situation.

Individuals both express and act-out feelings, and both behaviors have greater potential for causing disruption or progress. Individual responses can be unpredictable, and responses aren't always dependent on job security, organizational opportunities, rewards, or the effectiveness of the advance planning and communication.

Exploring requests for structural and assignment changes can provide an opportunity to learn what the employee understands and the reasons behind the request. The individual may be trying to move ahead, redress old grievances, or simply keep his or her balance. The ground is moving after a downsizing. That provides a wanted or unwanted opportunity for each employee to revise work plans and life plans. Some vulnerable employees will become quite distressed. It is essential to identify distress early and arrange optimal mental health evaluations.

Organizations are effective because they naturally enhance stability and inertia. Resistance to change is often supported by the well-oiled machine of organizational habits and patterns. Employee resistance can emerge in the form of irrelevant reports, pointless meetings, and routine expenditures.

Resistance can be visible in the behavior of both leaders and vulnerable employees. Leaders and vulnerable employees, in essence, are the canaries of the organization. Leaders may rely on habitual activities and responses to keep their balance and act as if nothing has happened. Many will work harder and sell more to show their worth. And they may get angry if this new dedication to work isn't appreciated. Other leaders may suppress dissent and become isolated or ineffective. In such cases, the leader's staff is left frightened and floundering.

Employee behavior may also signal something about group distress or organizational dysfunction. Employees with long-standing work or psychosocial difficulties may suddenly seem non-compliant or disinterested. Those vulnerable to emotional or physical distress are at a high risk of becoming poor performers or complainers. Routine problems can escalate to violence, fraud, or litigation. If there are many problematic employees in a particular work unit, then an organizational psychiatrist or other consultant can help.

How did the downsizing occur? The answer to this question has significant implications for the organization's range of responses. If the organization has been sold, for example, it's entirely possible that everyone is waiting for the other shoe to drop. In such a scenario, many marketable people will simply drift out of the organization if the situation is not well managed. If the downsizing is due to a merger, acquisition, or some other outside influence, the survivors may quickly form covert agendas and ties that can get in the way of new group goals. There's a high probability that the old group will take a "them vs. us" approach in coping with the change. These are the kinds of organizational gaps that HR must bridge.

Barriers to change will be especially high if the organization's downsizing is a result of poor performance. Feelings of incompetence foster very rigid ideas of what will and won't work. Employees are likely to rely on defensive responses. And if the group believes that separated employees were treated poorly, that won't be mitigated by positive vision statements. In that situation, survivors will be eager to show the new leaders how it used to be done.

Finding Solutions

Work relationships are not especially conducive to addressing feelings directly. It's a difficult task to convert feelings of distress and behavioral resistance into interest and productivity. But action must begin quickly or the group will lose energy and direction, or the demand for productivity will preempt proactive measures. At this stage, communication, behavior, timing, leadership, job definitions, and rewards best restore feelings of security and loyalty.

Communication

The rationale for new goals and structures must be clear and framed as employees are experiencing the problems. "We were losing money" or "the regulators demanded it," for example. Some, but not all, rumors are worth addressing. Don't be defensive or underestimate foolish rumors. Some foolish rumors turn out to be true.

Behavior

Don't assume that people know they're being resistant or unproductive. What's needed is specific direction, examples of what will be appreciated and tolerance for variety in how things get done. Vulnerable employees may need more structure or supervision. Problem employees need to be addressed early with structural limits. A lot of face time and evidence of external success are great ways to gain acceptance for the new priorities. Be reminded that good and bad behaviors are infectious. If you look distressed, many people will soon look just like you.

Timing

A speedy transition is a must. Groups read, with some accuracy, the mood and intentions of management. When decisions and promotions are planned, then delayed, the moment is lost. Decisions made after the delay are viewed as second best. In short, the lost moment is viewed as a leadership failure.

Leadership

There's no way to avoid distress, but there are ways to get the job done. Some leaders are best at increasing skills and teamwork. Others are better at riding the waves, attending to needs, and making people feel good about their contribution. Helping employees do what makes them feel competent mitigates distress. However, the accomplishments must be real. People quickly dismiss hype.

Job definitions and responsibilities need to be clarified early and with great sensitivity. Lack of definition can make the employee feel superfluous or threatened. However, excessive definition may be interpreted as a loss of power and potential. Everyone needs to feel they can sell their pet skills and ideas over time, in the new system.

Rewards

Rewards must be realigned to support goals. The bottom line is essential, but insufficient as a goal. Care must be given to define the variables that drive the bottom line such as job fit, access to resources, job satisfaction, skill sets and leadership. All require accurate reinforcement. Benchmarks need to be revisited. Simple measures of productivity that reflect both content and process can provide better feedback than turnover rates, complaints, or anonymous surveys.

Did It Help?

Revisit these issues regularly after a downsizing. Group writing and rewriting of the new vision, the new plan, and the new processes is the central device for assuring both understanding and commitment. Did it bring in diverse and useful ideas? Did it diffuse resistance and promote competence? Did good employees quit? Did production fall? Are there many retained employees who are obviously distressed? Did it get in the way of work? Were employees too busy to participate?

The need to be sensitive to people's feelings, especially in this situation, is not as much of a barrier to getting this job done as are the professional's own feelings—the fear of becoming involved and the distaste for messy interactions. Remember that mental states, even yours, are catching.

3 Managing a Downturn

Susan J. Wells

The best way to predict the future, it's been said, is to create it. It has also been said that if you can't make accurate predictions, be prepared to deal with all possible outcomes.

The human resource team at Capital One Financial Corp. tries to do both. Peering into the crystal ball takes the form of an information-based strategy used by HR professionals to link business trends with workforce planning.

Capital One, a credit card issuer and financial services company based in McLean, Virginia, asks managers directly to assess current workloads and what will drive staffing needs going forward. Using that information, HR then projects changes. On the basis of workload projections and anticipated productivity growth, the company quantifies the size of its required future workforce, allowing for adjustments.

These database simulations enable the company to forecast labor needs with greater precision and flexibility—which is especially helpful during times of economic uncertainty.

"This real-time scenario planning allows us to ebb and flow with the times—with much more flexibility in many of our business units," says Matt Schuyler, chief human resources officer of the 30,000-employee company. Without that model, he continues, "it's likely we would have experienced worse outcomes."

As the scope of the latest economic cycle plays out in 2008, it will be HR professionals' responsibility to help their organizations become more nimble in adapting to change. What they do today will position their organizations to look smart as business conditions improve—or, if they do nothing, they may be playing catch-up to their more agile competitors.

Tough Times Ahead

Capital One's strategy represents just one example of how employers seek smarter, smoother, steadier ways of managing their people assets through the inevitable ups and downs of the economy. Any threat of recession, of course, will adjust HR leaders' focus and priorities. But if they haven't prepared for the downside of the business cycle, they can find themselves ill-equipped. Too often, that means a scramble to plan and execute a recession-oriented HR strategy.

"Knee-jerk reactions to workforce needs are never well-received in an organization," Schuyler says. Instead, the ability to cope with any situation becomes the goal in successfully riding out a recession, workforce experts and economists say.

What is ultimately included in such contingency planning? Here is a rundown of some of the best guidance—a starting point and summary of ideas for weathering economic turbulence.

In the Gathering Storm

Steering an organization through a business downturn is never easy, but it can be an opportunity for HR professionals to help the enterprise thrive by maximizing core strengths—and minimizing weaknesses.

"Managing successfully through a recession is sometimes viewed almost as an art form," says Tamara Erickson, president of the Concours Institute, the Kingwood, Texas-based talent research and education arm of BSG Alliance Corp., a strategy consulting company. "If you have line managers in the business who have not weathered tough economic times in the past, provide them with coaching and mentoring by people who have."

Surviving a downturn involves judgment and a certain feel for what's happening, Erickson says—such as knowing how to distinguish between a true trend and a temporary blip and knowing when to take action and when to sit tight. "The trick is reading the signs well," she says.

Doing that means engaging in strategic discussions often and early, and sharpening your team's and your own financial acumen, Erickson says. Make sure everyone understands how your company makes money, how the financials can shift one way or the other, and how your business performs.

"Include a discussion of business performance and possible HR actions in every staff meeting," she says.

Then ask questions: What would you do if your company lost twenty percent of its revenue next quarter? Where would you focus cuts? What programs would you maintain or downsize? Would it challenge your talent strategy? Where would you cut, and where would you invest? Then, when a downturn looms, pull out the plan—and implement it.

At Houston-based Universal Weather and Aviation Inc., a provider of global support services for business aviation, Steve Ginsburgh, senior vice president of human resources and workforce development, takes a special approach: He uses a budget metric of human capital costs divided by the number of trip legs to calculate and forecast needs. Human capital costs include salaries, bonuses, benefits, consulting expenses, and temporary-worker costs. "When the ratio goes beyond our target, then we start to scrutinize hiring and add additional approvals to the process," he says. The economy's impact on the use of corporate aircraft usually relates to fuel prices and the degree to which global travel is regarded as necessary for business reasons, he explains.

Ginsburgh also identifies the roles most critical to keeping the business strong—and those that will be most important when the economy improves. "We are still looking at adding to compensation for critical customer-contact jobs for retention purposes," he says. "And we'll always look for opportunities to seek great new employees. Our customers expect perfect trips from us, and cutting staff is not the way to do it."

Survey the Landscape

A slowdown can be a good time to examine your workforce's underlying potential, says Pat Chadbourne, director of APAC Associates Inc., a workforce planning and consulting firm in Charlotte, North Carolina. It can be a time to find out who's waiting in the wings, a time "to build up bench strength and identify the 'sleepers' out there." They may include "those who have previous experience and skills that [the company] can tap," she explains, or retirees "with special expertise who can be enticed to come back in at critical times."

To best manage the uncertainty about talent needs, companies should constantly calculate the "short and long," advises Peter Cappelli, professor of management at the Wharton School, University of Pennsylvania, and director of Wharton's Center for Human Resources. Cappelli is also author of *Talent on Demand: Managing Talent in an Age of Uncertainty*.[1]

"Suppose a company forecasts that it will need 100 new engineers this year," Cappelli says. "Not many people ask the question 'How accurate is that forecast?' As it turns out, that forecast is almost always wrong because business needs are so hard to predict. So the way to proceed is to ask, 'What happens if we are wrong?'"

HR can be wrong in one of two ways: Either you end up needing fewer engineers than you thought you would, and you have to carry them or lay them off, he says, or you need more engineers than you thought, and you have to scramble to find extras.

According to Cappelli, the next question should be "'What does that cost us in each case? Does it cost us more if we have too many, or if we have too few?' It's almost always the case that it is much worse in one context than in the other."

Communicating with Employees

Ironically, internal communication between managers and employees tends to decrease as business declines, says Brian Wilkerson, practice director for talent management in the Denver office of HR consulting firm Watson Wyatt Worldwide.

Wilkerson instead recommends that a company quickly and specifically tailor communication to key employee groups. As soon as the "R word"—recession—is in the wind, upper managers and the HR team should pull together the top five percent of employees to discuss the business plan and to outline their commitment to these key employees.

"Engage them early on and express their value to the company," Wilkerson says. "Making it clear to top performers that you want them to be a part of the solutions now and the better times ahead can go a long way in rallying to the cause and keeping the best and brightest."

Keeping lines of communication open helps HR develop the supportive organizational culture that breeds loyalty among employees and an uncommon willingness to sacrifice for the company in tough times, says Peter Navarro, professor of economics and public policy at the Paul Merage School of Business at the University of California-Irvine. This culture-building focus helps HR leaders find alternatives to layoffs and win support for labor-preserving, cost-cutting moves, as Navarro describes in his book, *The Well-Timed Strategy: Managing the Business Cycle for Competitive Advantage.*[2] The book contains analyses of hundreds of companies' efforts to manage through economic recessions and expansions.

Such tactics, Navarro says, helped Nucor Corp., a 17,300-employee steel producer based in Charlotte, North Carolina, implement a flexible "Share the Pain" program. The program enables the company to taper labor costs in recessions without loss of productive capacity by using a progressive scale of reduced hours or wages and by shifting its highly flexible and cross-trained workforce to other functions as needed.

A sharper focus on productivity and redeployment also drives HR efforts in slowdowns. High on the agenda should be retention efforts to ward off the higher turnover expected as the economic recovery takes hold, Navarro says.

In advance of the 2001 recession, for example, HR strategy at Xilinx Inc., a semiconductor chip designer in San Jose, California, focused squarely on employee retention, Navarro points out. Instead of layoffs, the company responded to the downturn with salary reductions, mandatory vacations, and a yearlong sabbatical program that paid employees a small stipend if they went to school or worked for nonprofits. The lowest-paid workers suffered no pay cuts, while the chief executive officer's salary was reduced by twenty percent and his bonus was eliminated.

The "protective HR umbrella alleviated employees' fears that they or their teammates might lose their jobs," Navarro says, "leaving the workers better able to focus on product innovation." Xilinx's gambit yielded more than $35 million in labor savings. Moreover, as the economy and the chip sector began to recover in 2002, the strategy let the company roll out a suite of innovative products in each of three categories, thereby grabbing market share from competitors.

Getting Ready for Recovery

A slowdown can be the time to consider targeted recruitment. In the depths of a recession, the last thing many leaders want to do is hire more people, Navarro says. "But it's precisely at the trough of a recession that the labor pool is at its deepest and highest quality. Moreover, any wage pressures will have totally subsided. That's why a recession is a great time to cherry-pick."

Strategically adding and upgrading staff better positions employers for economic recovery, enabling them to gain a critical competitive advantage. When economic expansion begins, those companies deploy a more highly skilled workforce with lower labor costs than rivals, Navarro says. He cites two examples.

Progressive Insurance, a major automobile insurer based in Mayfield Village, Ohio, recruits on college campuses during recessions to sign up and train high-quality students anxious about finding employment after graduation.

Isis Pharmaceuticals, a drug discovery and development company in Carlsbad, California, leverages downturns in the biotechnology industry to lock top scientific talent into long-term positions at bargain salaries.

A slowdown also can heighten the value of developing existing talent. In 2004, for example, Capital One launched a Career Development Center to assess, counsel, and retrain displaced employees for work in other units. Two years later, the company opened the service to all employees seeking career development or change. Through physical locations and an online presence, the internal center supported 8,400 employees in 2007 alone. "Ideally," says HR chief Schuyler, "we want our folks to stay with us, if they prefer to."

4 Riding Out the Storm with Clear Explanations

Steve Taylor

When the economy turns soft, companies often lay off employees or shorten their work hours. Morale plummets as workers who keep their jobs feel frightened and resentful, if not angry. But the company still needs their best efforts—needs them more than ever, in fact. And it often falls to employee relations professionals to keep everyone working together.

A hard trick to pull off? "You just don't know!" declares Nachelle Rantin, PHR, whose employer, Ashley Furniture, a manufacturer, wholesaler and retailer headquartered in Arcadia, Wisconsin, has been rocked by the sinking housing and mortgage industries. "No one is buying homes. Therefore, they do not need furniture," Rantin explains. "We have had to reduce staffing between twenty and thirty percent over the last 90 days," at the Ashley warehouse center in Fairburn, Georgia, where Rantin is area HR manager. "We've had to go to reduced work schedules, obviously with no overtime at all."

Also in Fairburn, near Atlanta, LaRhonda Edwards, PHR, DDI, is a division HR manager for U.S. Foodservice. "Most of our employees are used to 40-hour, full-time jobs," she says. "We tell our associates that our new expectation is to get them at least 36 hours." When they object, Edwards says, she gives workers examples of worse economic troubles elsewhere, such as layoffs and shutdowns, and asks, "Would you rather have fewer hours or no jobs at all?"

Edwards is an advocate of giving workers clear explanations of the reasons behind the cuts. "We have town hall meetings," she reports, "where everybody, all employees gather together to hear business updates…We talk very directly about what's going on."

"This is a food service business," she continues. "We deliver to restaurants, and eating out is a luxury that people can do without. That means less orders coming in, less production. We talk honestly about this being a soft economy." She claims that when employees hear the whole story, they generally understand and accept. "It's one of those 'Aha!' moments. They say, 'You're right, we would rather lose four hours than lose them all.'"

The newspaper business has suffered from an economy-driven slump in advertising on top of years of declining readership. In Stuart, Florida, HR Director Janice Green says her employer, Scripps Treasure Coast Newspapers, is doing better than some other companies. "We've really had only a handful of individual layoffs, 12 over six months. Through attrition we've eliminated some more positions." Even so, she says, department directors have had regular meetings with workers to explain the situation and talk it through. "To allow people to be scared" is how Green characterizes it. "[The fear] has to come out. It's not good to suppress it." She says publisher Tom Weber "has been very honest with employees. To sugarcoat at this point would not be very wise."

At Ashley Furniture, "We did a state-of-the-business meeting in all of our stores," reports Rantin. Managers gathered all employees together, "trying to keep everyone feeling they have some type of security in that we just have to weather the storm, remain positive, stay a team."

Consultant Jodi Starkman, COO, Global Consulting for ORC Worldwide, talks about "improving business literacy" among workers: "Sharing information about the cost of employment, so employees understand total compensation cost. What it costs for you to be here. This makes people more sensitive."

In addition to face-to-face meetings, Starkman says, virtual town halls are becoming more common. "A lot of companies have employee [web] portals where leaders share information. Not just e-mails, but video presentations." One purpose, she adds, is "so that everyone receives the information at the same time and in the same way."

Starkman says savvy employee relations professionals tailor these top-down communications for specific audiences so that workers "have the information they need without details that could be overwhelming or potentially misconstrued … Employees on an assembly line don't necessarily need the same information as managers. But they need information," she stresses, because when an uninformed employee draws his or her own conclusion about a company's financial condition, "it's invariably worse" than the truth.

Bottom Up

As companies tighten their belts, surviving workers often must take on more responsibility and work. And they may be called upon to send critical information upward to management. U.S. Foodservice is using "round-table meetings," says Edwards, with "one designated person from each department to offer suggestions." She said that during that process, employees came up with one idea that managers had feared might be resisted. "They said, 'Oh, can we work a four-day week?' They were already on board with it. They'd bought in to it."

Jeffrey Fina of New York's Michael C. Fina Co., which provides corporations with employee recognition programs, says the classic suggestion-box approach still works well in "getting the employees engaged, really developing the team atmosphere."

ORC's Starkman says, "Historically, the focus has always been on what to do to control costs." In addition, she says, there is "an opportunity that HR has been missing out on" at many companies: "Moving away from [only] reducing costs to revenue enhancement, value creation activities."

Fina advises that HR challenge employees to make clear and practical suggestions for specific areas of company need. "It has to be an operating efficiency suggestion," he says. "Why do you think this would create increased efficiency in our operations? How do you propose to implement it and what will the results be? Not just blurting out suggestions."

Rewards

And when the suggestions are good? Janice Green of Scripps Treasure Coast Newspapers says three employees have received company awards recently. Ashley Furniture's Nachelle Rantin says, "We have a recognition and reward program in place, but we've had to cut that back as well."

"Companies need to hunker down and watch every penny," acknowledges Fina, "but they also need to realize that their employees are their most valuable asset. You can't stop investing in that asset."

Starkman says, "Somewhere along the way there has to be recognition that new ideas lead to new revenue." She suggests that employees who contribute to that process should be compensated with bonuses and made into role models for other workers. "Those are the kinds of people we reward, the leaders we want."

5 Many Plan To Scale Back Benefits, Pay Raises as Economy Slows

Stephen Miller

Many U.S. companies are preparing to make big changes to their salaries and benefits structures, as well as to their planned staffing levels, in the event of a sustained recession, according to a new study by Hay Group.[1] The consulting firm surveyed approximately 250 HR compensation executives and CEOs across all industries for its Slowing Economy Spot Survey.

There's no doubt that the growth of the U.S. economy has slowed in recent months. According to a U.S. Department of Labor report,[2] employers worried about recession slashed 80,000 jobs in March 2008, the most in five years and the third consecutive month of losses. Also signaling economic contraction: the national unemployment rate rose to 5.1 percent from 4.8 percent.

In his testimony before Congress in April 2008, Federal Reserve Chairman Ben S. Bernanke said that "it now appears likely that real gross domestic product will not grow much, if at all, over the first half of 2008 and could even contract slightly."[3]

Still, it remains unclear whether an actual recession (typically defined as two consecutive quarters of falling real gross national product) would be short-lived or lingering. Because of this economic uncertainty, "Most companies are likely conducting an analysis of the business forecast for the next quarter, as well as pinpointing how market compensation practices should change during this downward economic cycle," observes Tom McMullen, vice president at Hay Group and one of the leaders of the study.

Freezing Salaries and Staffing

Regarding compensation and staffing levels, the Hay Group study indicates that:

- More than 30 percent of surveyed companies are freezing or considering freezing base salaries.
- 15 percent are freezing salaries for all employees.
- 20 percent say they will be freezing or decreasing staffing levels in the near future.

Most of the respondents reported that executive, management, and professional groups are most at risk for salary freezes—while there is a lower prevalence of freezing or considering freezing base salaries for skilled trade and support/clerical groups.

"Short of layoffs or salary cuts, this is as serious as you can get in terms of sending out distress signals," says McMullen.

Trimming Benefits

Regarding employee benefits, the study indicates that:

- Employer-provided benefits are being put under the microscope, especially when it comes to health care—27 percent report they have either made changes or are making changes to health care benefits.
- 20 percent indicated that they have changes either implemented or planned for retirement/pension benefits.
- 28 percent indicated that they have changes implemented or planned for training and development programs.

Retention Still Matters

That said, when companies were asked about their primary concerns regarding engaging and retaining key employees during challenging economic periods, they identified retaining and motivating their key contributors as their number one concern. The "balancing act" in a sustained recession, according to Hay Group's analysis, will be to restrain overall rewards budgets while sparing the most-valued employees as much pain as possible.

6 As Staffing Slips, Recruiters Must Work Harder

Theresa Minton-Eversole

Staffing industry employment declined slightly in the first quarter of 2008 compared to the same period in 2007, according to survey data released in May 2008, by the American Staffing Association (ASA).[1]

America's staffing companies employed an average of 2.8 million temporary and contract workers per day from January through March—down 1.7 percent, or 48,000 jobs, from the first quarter of 2007, according to the ASA Staffing Index. The index, which measures weekly changes in staffing industry employment, has been flat since the beginning of the year.

"Demand has softened for lower skilled labor, but there continues to be growing demand for higher skilled talent," said ASA President and Chief Executive Officer Richard Wahlquist in a statement. However, he said, "The latest data suggest that the staffing industry has remained more resilient than in previous periods when the economy had slowed and we had precipitous drops in temporary and contract employment."

U.S. sales of temporary and contract staffing totaled $17.7 billion in the first quarter of 2008, an increase of 1.5 percent over the same quarter of the previous year, and a new first quarter record, according to the ASA survey.

Still, the labor market in general is much weaker in June 2008 than it was a year ago and will continue to be soft, with a sharp decline in employment expectations in manufacturing and service sector jobs, according to the 2008 Society for Human Resource Management (SHRM)/Rutgers LINE survey report.[2]

The Leading Indicators of National Employment (LINE) report shows that for June 2008:

- Far fewer hires likely will be made, based on a substantial drop in employment expectations for the service sector (down 28.2 points) and manufacturing (down 11.1 points) compared to one year ago.
- Mixed compensation growth is expected for new hires. The much larger service sector fell significantly compared to May 2007; manufacturing will increase modestly in new-hire compensation.
- The difficulty of recruiting lessened substantially for manufacturing and service sectors compared to May 2007 levels.

Tighten, Don't Trash, Staffing Strategies

The fact that recruiting difficulty has lessened doesn't mean employment professionals are coasting down easy street. In fact, some experts say it's quite the contrary.

"It's always important for companies to hire the best people, whether it's in a down economy or a thriving economy," said Jeremy Eskenazi, founding principal of Long Beach, California-based global human resources consulting firm Riviera Advisors. "But in a down economy, it becomes even more difficult to find A-level talent because those employees are being coveted and retained by employers. What's more, A-level employees are less open to changing jobs in a slow market because of the uncertainty that comes with today's economy."

As such, he said, "Recruiters and employers need to be more strategic and creative in how they find and attract top talent today. What may have worked a year ago, will not work today."

Eskenazi said recruiters and companies need to be looking at a whole spectrum of ideas, including better severance packages, richer or more flexible relocation options, and virtual work arrangements, among others. In addition, companies need to have policies and procedures in place so recruiters can sell their open positions effectively.

"Today recruiters need to sell 'safety' and 'security' when talking to candidates about the job openings they have," he said. "If they don't have the tools to sell safety and security, they won't be effective."

Many companies see a down market as an opportunity to acquire talent, beat back competition, grow market share, gain a competitive advantage, or restructure their organization to better meet their business needs, he added. "The media covers a lot of the 'doom and gloom' about a down economy, but smart companies and recruitment leaders see opportunities and are positioning themselves for when the eventual rebound comes."

For example, some forward-thinking companies in housing-related industries are continuing to grow their talent management activities, as are some companies in the hospitality industry, which is feeling the ripple effects of the economic slowdown and high gas prices.

"There is nervousness and pessimism about the economy and its effects on [this] industry, but we have not seen widespread or rampant layoffs," said Diana M. Meisenhelter, also a principal with Riviera. "At this point, companies are definitely being very conservative with their HR spending. If there is any good news, it's that the hospitality industry is used to economic downturns. In fact, this economic downturn is nothing compared to 2001."

Adds Meisenhelter: "From a strategic staffing and recruiting standpoint, the smart hospitality HR executives, talent management, and recruitment leaders know that this is one area they cannot neglect, because when the economy picks back up, they need to be ready to fill any and all open positions. Mapping to where you are now and where you will be in the future is critical."

Eskenazi and Meisenhelter say the best companies are doing three things right now:

1. They have a solid, proactive sourcing plan that drives actual results in candidates being acquired.
2. They have a proactive recruiting plan to build a pipeline of top candidates that can be tapped into before they are needed.
3. They are focusing on internal movement; using the talent they already have at their organizations to fill positions.

"The best companies we talk to do a great job of rallying their employees," said Meisenhelter. "[They] continue to recognize their new and existing employees in a unique, memorable and meaningful way. They could be cutting back on these 'soft' priorities but they're not, and this can help with retention in a big way."

Meisenhelter said it's important for HR professionals to maintain a cool head and not overreact to the current economic climate by deeply cutting back on staffing or scaling back on talent management acquisition priorities.

"You still need to hire the best talent you can, and if you're not, your competition will," she said. "Smart companies realize this and are using this time as an opportunity to find great people and build their candidate pipelines."

It's also a great time for HR professionals to really assess the effectiveness of their staffing and recruiting functions, she added.

"They should be asking questions like, 'How can we streamline operations,' 'Where can we save money and resources?', 'What's the most high-value activity we should be focused on?' and 'How can we show return on investment?'"

"In a down economy where money is tight and budgets are being cut," she said, "showing ROI is probably one of the most important functions you can do."

7 Recruiting Grads

Theresa Minton-Eversole

Employers are ramping up for the spring college recruitment season, and early indications point to a good job market with higher starting salaries than last year for the Class of 2008, according to the latest quarterly salary survey results published by the National Association of Colleges and Employers (NACE).[1]

But campus recruiters are going to be facing a future workforce that is made up of workers who are as concerned about what the company can do for them as they are about how they might contribute to the company's success.

Although early data are limited, the overall average starting salary offer reported in the winter issue of the NACE Salary Survey is four percent higher than the average starting salary offer in winter 2007.

"It is important to recognize that this overall average masks some variations among different academic disciplines and among majors within those disciplines," said Edwin Koc, NACE director of strategic and foundation research. "Still, at this early juncture, our data suggest that new college graduates are in demand."

Two-Way or No-Way Demands

Among the business disciplines, marketing graduates are expected to enjoy healthy starting salaries that are, on average, five percent higher in 2007, bringing the average salary offer to $43,459. On the other hand, accounting, finance, and business administration/management graduates—also expected to draw starting salaries in the mid- to upper $40s—will see increases of only one to two percent.

Many graduates with technical degrees, including computer science and engineering, also are drawing higher starting salaries, with average percentage increases ranging from 3.5 percent to as much as nearly eight percent, depending on the specialty area. And, as a group, liberal arts graduates started the year on a high note with a nine percent increase, bringing their average starting salary offer to $33,258.

Such salaries might initially get graduates' attention, but new survey research by Experience Inc., a Boston career services firm for college students, shows that employers that share what else their company can do for these potential employees will have an even greater impact on graduates and a higher likelihood of hiring them.

In Experience Inc.'s 2007 Job Description Survey, results of which were released February 2008, a majority of college students and recent grads agreed that companies do not do a good job of communicating key information such as corporate ethics and reputation, career advancement, and training opportunities in their job descriptions.[2]

For the survey, 117 students and recent grads from 35 states reviewed actual job descriptions from five global companies across a variety of industries. Respondents evaluated these blind job postings based on their effectiveness in communicating the position, its requirements and benefits for prospective employees.

Eighty-three percent of respondents said the companies were good at describing basic job qualifications and responsibilities, and seventy-two percent said they did a good job explaining how a position fits with the applicant's skills. But the results also showed there is a clear gap between what members of the Millennial generation value in a job and what employers included in their job descriptions.

Fifty-four percent of respondents rated the companies' communication about their ethics and reputation as fair to poor, while fifty-five percent rated communication about career opportunities as such. In addition, sixty-four percent of respondents rated the companies' communication about training opportunities as fair to poor.

"Our research shows that many organizations need to reassess how they write their job descriptions, changing from what companies want to a description that better explains how the position will benefit candidates," said Jennifer Floren, founder and CEO of Experience Inc. "Providing information about career advancement, professional development and work/life balance will help employers stand out among the competition."

Among the tips cited in Experience Inc.'s white paper, "It's Time for a Job Description Makeover,"[3] to make job descriptions more effective:

- Make job descriptions succinct and understandable, including company overview and industry information, as well as a description of the employee's role within the organization and key reporting relationships.
- Include details such as the number of hours expected per week, basic duties and responsibilities with percentages of time allocated to each, and the amount of travel associated with the position.
- Share stories of how employees in similar positions progressed if career path information is not available.
- Be specific when listing benefits (e.g., note tuition reimbursement amount).

8 Address Financial Ills To Reduce Other Workplace Problems

Rebecca R. Hastings, SPHR

Employer efforts to help employees address financial challenges might lessen the side effects financial stress can have on the workplace.

"Financial problems are toxic," said Reeta Wolfsohn of the Center for Financial Social Work during a June 2008, Employee Assistance Professionals (EAP) Association webinar. "They manifest themselves in every area of a person's existence, corrupting their home and work life, their relationships, their thinking, and their behavior."

When the economy is unbalanced, employees might experience a wide range of spillover effects, including bankruptcy, foreclosure, car or boat repossession, high medical bills, and/or ten to twelve maxed out credit cards, she said. Some might be going through a divorce settlement linked to the financial problems they've experienced.

Wolfsohn said employees with financial problems might not be able to pay child support or child care, take a vacation, keep up with mortgage or rent payments, contribute to a retirement account, or cover college expenses.

Employers can watch for warning signs that an employee is under financial stress such as absenteeism and tardiness, reduced productivity and accuracy, and requests to change or eliminate 401(k) contributions.

Wolfsohn said employees might be more confrontational, distracted, irritable, and less reliable, patient, and dependable. They might even engage in high-risk or illegal behavior such as gambling, self-medicating, embezzlement, or theft.

Financial stress can manifest itself in health issues such as high blood pressure, insomnia, depression, anxiety, and weight gain, she added.

It Can Happen to Anyone

According to Wolfsohn, forty percent of employees say they have financial problems, and eighty percent of financially stressed workers spend time at work dealing with or worrying about money.

And Wolfsohn said employees might unwittingly increase their debt load by failing to pay a bill on time as a result of "universal default" that allows all of an individual's creditors to raise interest rates to as high as thirty-four percent if they are one day late on a payment to a single creditor.

Such an outcome is understandable when one considers that the average credit card debt per American household is $9,200, according to Wolfsohn, and the average interest rate on credit cards is 19.2 percent. This is why seventy-five percent of Americans are reportedly just three paychecks away from bankruptcy.

Tackling the Problem

EAP professionals participating in the webinar noted they have seen a significant increase in the number of employees with financial problems. The key to solving such problems, according to Wolfsohn, lies not in an understanding of finance but in an understanding of behavior.

"It doesn't matter if you make $20,000 or $120,000, if you are spending more than you make," she said. That's why employers need to find ways to reach employees who are not contacting the EAP for help. "There's a tremendous amount of shame and isolation," she says, particularly for those with high incomes.

Financial social work focuses on personal awareness as much as financial awareness. Wolfsohn likened it to substance abuse treatment or weight loss support: "Until and unless behavior changes, nothing changes."

However, some EAPs take a reactive approach to employee financial challenges, a strategy Wolfsohn discouraged.

"A reactive approach doesn't understand how much employee's financial problems and stress impact the workplace environment and the company's bottom line," she said. As a result, EAP counselors might simply refer clients to consumer credit counseling services or bankruptcy attorneys.

But these services have downsides, according to Wolfsohn: "Neither one of these offers any kind of behavioral model for change," she says, and both experience high recidivism rates. Moreover, she said, the reactive approach "doesn't take into account how dangerous and unstable employees with financial problems and stress are to themselves, to their families, their colleagues, and the workplace."

A proactive approach begins with a company culture that supports employee efforts to become more money-wise, Wolfsohn said. Such companies realize that employees who are financially stable are typically emotionally stable. And this, she said, affects the company's bottom line as much as it benefits an employee's personal life.

Employers can start by increasing their awareness of the problem and by educating themselves and their employees about the risks associated with overreliance on credit cards. They should make every effort to create an environment in which employees feel safe talking about money, Wolfsohn said.

In addition, Wolfsohn suggested that EAP professionals routinely ask all clients, whether they are seeking financial help or not, to identify their level of credit card and other debt when they complete an intake questionnaire. This can help identify employees who are at risk before a situation becomes unmanageable.

"People need education, motivation and support to make the choice to take greater responsibility for their own financial future," Wolfsohn said, adding that employees must understand that how they spend their money reflects their values.

"Remember that financial problems and issues are enduring, long-term challenges, not one-time events," she concluded. "If the behavior doesn't change there will be future problems."

9 Prune Employees Carefully

Adrienne Fox

Many companies in diverse industries face the economic downturn by cutting their largest expense: head count.

In the United States, January 2008 layoffs rose a whopping sixty-nine percent from December 2007 to 75,000—the highest amount since August 2007, according to outplacement firm Challenger, Gray and Christmas in Chicago. Housing and financial sectors were hit hardest, confirm Challenger officials.

The rest of 2008 looks just as ugly, according to Career Protection's Annual 2008 Layoffs Forecast survey of 1,375 corporate executives nationwide conducted in January.[1] The survey predicts a thirty-seven percent increase in layoffs this year compared to last, making this year's forecast the worst in five years.

"This year, you will see a breadth of industries predicting layoffs," including automotive, pharmaceutical, retail, leisure, and hospitality industries, as well as professional and technical services, says Kirk Nemer, SPHR, president and chief executive officer of Denver-based Career Protection, an employee-focused human resources and legal consulting firm.

Managers in many HR departments are in the midst of planning for or conducting layoffs, Nemer reports. He has advice for those who haven't yet received the call from chief financial officers looking for ways to cut staff: Be prepared.

"Corporations are going to have to get leaner," he predicts. "There will be more layoffs throughout the year."

To determine if your company is at risk, "study your business and your industry," advises Nemer, adding: If hard times have come or are forecast, work with managers to determine parts of the business that can slash staff or cut operations, as defined by the business plan. Then, turn to the performance management system and reviews to determine employees who can be let go. Nemer counsels HR professionals to:

- Make sure appraisals are up-to-date.
- Identify top performers and get them working on the company's future.
- Have leaders committed to the company's turnaround.

In short, have faith in your performance management system, never lose sight of the big picture—and retain top talent.

The Groundwork

A robust performance management system constitutes the first piece of the layoff puzzle that should be in place long before managers contemplate job cuts. Unfortunately, that's not the reality, experts find.

"Organizations do themselves a disservice when they don't have a rigorous performance management system that supports HR decisions, particularly around layoffs," says Matt Angello, founder of Bright Tree Consulting Group in Lancaster, Pennsylvania, and former vice president of HR at Armstrong World Industries.

"If you don't have a vigorous performance management system, you don't have an operating plan; you have an operating hope," says Angello. And when it comes time to select people for layoffs, your decisions are based on guesswork rather than fact, he adds. "You get into a fuzzy area where managers start picking those who look like them to stay," opening up the company to legal risks.

Bob Kustka, founder of HR consultancy The Fusion Factor in Norwell, Massachusetts, says companies that "don't closely manage their performance appraisal systems suddenly learn during a reduction in force that everyone has been ranked a 'four' out of 'five,'" says Kustka. "That information is meaningless."

Managers should conduct workforce planning in advance, he adds. "You should always look at the demographics of your workforce and ask, 'Do I have the right number of people? Do I have the right competencies?'"

Kustka recalls the workforce planning he conducted as an HR executive at The Gillette Company. "Technology was a core competency and we relied on experienced engineers [at Gillette]," he says. In the early 1990s,

"We had a lot of 50-year-old experienced engineering talent in the middle and didn't have a feeder system. We had put hiring on hold for six years [in the 1980s], and that was the result."

Deep cuts or long-term hiring freezes during this economic slump could come back to haunt companies trying to compete long term, as it did at Gillette, says Kustka.

If you haven't been engaged in workforce planning and your chief financial officer calls for a major reduction in force, a big-picture mind-set becomes helpful. While belt-tightening may be the order of the day, in the near future, with baby boomers retiring, you will need top talent.

Leaner Staffing

Leaders of many organizations have been staffing smarter in recent years, perhaps having learned the hard lesson of the 2001-2002 shallow recession that rebounded into a competitive labor market soon after.

Kustka has seen many such economic cycles, but forecasts a different scenario this time: "Companies are making reductions in force, but [managers] are much more concerned this time around about how they make those reductions because talent has been harder to get," he says.

As early as 2006, companies started slowing their hiring activities, when the number of positions filled decreased twenty-three percent from the previous year, according to the Society for Human Resource Management's (SHRM) *Human Capital Benchmarking Study: 2007 Executive Summary*. A shift was also noted when the SHRM/Rutgers University Leading Indicators of National Employment (LINE) index showed a downward turn in hiring expectations in fall 2007. According to the March 2008 LINE report, hiring for the manufacturing and service sectors will be down sharply.[2]

Companies are leaner than in recessions past, according to experts, because of the proliferation of worldwide mergers and acquisitions, outsourcing, and the "rightsizing" management philosophy that eliminated redundancies in positions.

Nuera Communications Inc., a provider of voice-over-Internet-protocol infrastructure solutions in San Diego, is a product of "rightsizing" after being acquired in 2006 by Israel-based AudioCodes, a communications company.

AudioCodes reduced Nuera's workforce from more than 200 employees to roughly 40. "It's been painful," says Mike Rinehart, vice president of business operations for North America at AudioCodes. He handled HR for

Nuera before the acquisition.

AudioCodes' leaders wanted to eliminate redundant positions, "so some of the senior manager positions were cut," recalls Rinehart. The companies had similar product lines, and AudioCodes discontinued developing Nuera's products. That gave rise to reductions in research and development (R&D) positions and some manufacturing operations in North America. The consolidation led to layoffs.

Streamlining as a result of the acquisition was a "healthy process," says Rinehart. But in the first quarter of 2007, AudioCodes didn't meet Wall Street's profit expectations, and leaders looked at further consolidation—and job cuts—in financial, manufacturing, and R&D.

That consolidation process wasn't clear, causing problems when AudioCodes' leaders didn't communicate well. "Being based in another country didn't help communication," says Rinehart. "It's gotten better over time. But in a situation like layoffs, you need to over-communicate."

Say It Often

Once you have decided to reduce your force, how you communicate and when you communicate are key. "Don't put a rosy spin on it," says Kustka. "And don't be afraid to go to employees when you don't have all the answers. Employees find out about it right away and get concerned."

That was Rinehart's experience at Nuera. "Turnover was high because of the angst about what AudioCodes was going to do and not knowing what the future held," he says.

A similar sense of uncertainty spurs calls to Nemer from employees at Sprint, Bear Stearns, and Citigroup, among others that have announced layoffs.

"Employees are shocked and scared," he reports. "We're even getting calls from people who are hearing rumors of possible layoffs at the end of the year, and they're asking what they can do to protect themselves. We tell them to continue to perform at a high level because no matter how stressed the economy gets, companies still need top performers."

The rumor mill undermines morale and can put top performers at risk, Angello warns.

Retain Top Talent

Indeed, companies need top performers. Corporate leaders can't assume that because the economy may tank—and workers seemingly have no place else to go—employees won't try to jump ship.

It may seem oxymoronic to focus on retention when conducting layoffs, but there's no other time when retention becomes more paramount than when a company lets workers go.

HR professionals need "to get in front of the line managers and critically assess [who] is the talent they must retain," says Timothy Brown, SPHR, manager of staffing at CertainTeed Corporation, a Pottstown, Pennsylvania, and *Fortune* 100 company. "Ensure that you have some capability in place to help the talent be part of the solution."

Rinehart says turnover at Nuera stabilized when team members were given a defined role in the turnaround after the layoffs. "Those teams that had a part in meeting the company's goals were focused and productive," he explains.

AudioCodes redeployed top performers if they worked in areas where there was redundancy or product elimination. "There were some retention bonuses, but I personally believe that money doesn't retain top talent," says Rinehart. "You have to give them more of a reason to stay by finding a meaningful role for that person where he or she can contribute to the success of the organization and have room for growth."

Brown agrees: "While you retain the person, you won't necessarily retain the spirit or the will to contribute. The key is to help the retained folks have a part in enabling the turnaround."

Brown challenges employees to come up with strategies to help the company rebound. "Encourage entrepreneurial spirit among your employees and challenge them to find new opportunities," he says. "See how they respond. In times of trouble, how employees respond really separates your leaders from the rest of the pack."

Ready for Rebound

Economists disagree on whether the country is in a recession, or will go into a recession, or how long a recession will last.

"Typically, once a recession is announced, you're almost out of it," says Brown. "You have to be ready to rebound."

To ward against future layoffs, leaders of the 600-employee AudioCodes remain cautious about growth. The strategy: "Make sure to not hire too many people when times are good," says Rinehart. "We are very careful about who we hire so that we have the right people ready when we need them to take on leadership roles."

10 Reduction in Force and Employees with Performance Problems

Can employers include employees who have performance problems in a reduction in force (RIF)? Yes, if the employer has solid written documentation of the business purpose for the RIF, as well as defendable reasons for how and why employees were chosen for layoff.

After a company has determined that a RIF is the best way to meet the financial goals for the business, a business analysis should be conducted to determine the employees who will be affected. Nondiscriminatory employee selection criteria should be developed and used to select the employees who will be laid off.

Performance criteria may be used and employers may consider previous performance reviews and other performance documentation, such as warnings or any type of disciplinary actions. Employers may also wish to use seniority as a determining factor.

However, a RIF is based on a business need to cut costs or to better align resources so the business is able to meet overall goals and objectives—and it is not the best way to manage performance issues. Laying off employees with performance problems, who are in necessary positions, may create problems for the company. The employer will need to fill the positions, and this could lead to claims of wrongful discharge or discrimination.

Using a RIF to manage performance can also lead to morale problems with staff who remain employed. Employees often can see when their peers have performance problems. When strong-performing employees find out that poor-performing employees received severance payments and management didn't address the performance issues, it can lead to decreased respect toward managers, as well as waning employer loyalty and increased turnover.

11 Employers Using Benefits To Help Employees Fill the Tank

As gasoline prices continue to rise, more employers are offering additional benefits, such as telecommuting and flexible schedules, to help offset those costs, according to a May 2008 Society for Human Resource Management (SHRM) survey.

Most organizations are using benefits, not increased pay, to help employees cope. Only two percent of surveyed employers offered a cost of living raise prompted by gas prices, or stipends to employees with long commutes. Instead, employers are offering new benefits, and more employees are taking advantage of benefits they already had.

The survey report, *What Employers Are Doing to Help Their Employees with High Gas Prices in 2008*, showed that the most common tactic (42 percent) was to raise the mileage reimbursement to the IRS maximum. Other benefits include offering a flexible work schedule (26 percent), telecommuting (18 percent), public transportation discounts (14 percent), and rewarding employee performance with a gas card (14 percent).[1]

"Rising gas prices are cutting into everyone's personal budgets, so employees are taking a closer look at benefits such as compressed work weeks and public transportation discounts to reduce their costs," says Susan R. Meisinger, SPHR, former president and CEO of SHRM. "In addition, employers are offering extra help as a tool to retain employees and improve employee morale."

Other key survey findings include:

- Driving-related assistance has risen dramatically. For example, 13 percent of employers raised mileage reimbursement to the IRS cap in

2007, compared to 42 percent this year.

- Some employers (12 percent) assist employees organize carpools, and 7 percent offer priority parking to employees who carpool.
- Other benefits: offering new non-executive hires help in finding housing closer to the office (4 percent) and offering a monetary incentive for employees to buy hybrid cars (1 percent).

12 Tighter Times, Leaner Technology

Jennifer Taylor Arnold

Whether you call today's economic problems a downturn, an adjustment, or a recession, the economy clearly is generating trouble. But that trouble doesn't have to derail your HR technology strategy. Tough times and leaner budgets can actually prompt you to get more value from your technology dollars, HR professionals and consultants say.

Hunt for functions your current software contains but you don't use. Negotiate more effectively with your current HR technology vendors. Tinker with systems to re-purpose them for new uses—perhaps handling HR tasks related to job cuts. These and other ideas can help HR squeeze services and functions from vendors and products.

"We're hearing anecdotally that industries across the board are hunkering down" on HR technology spending, says Michael Cornetto, a New York-based senior strategy consultant for HR service delivery for consultant Watson Wyatt Worldwide. "By the end of this year, next year's budgets will be much tighter."

At Capital One, a financial services company based in McLean, Virginia, Douglas Krey, senior vice president for HR, says HR technology budget requests for 2008 were about ten percent lower than in the past few years. He attributes the drop-off partly to pressures from the economy and partly to a tapering off from large investments in technology in 2004-2006.

Smart Shopping

Tight budgets don't necessarily mean a halt in spending. A tougher economy might prompt some employers to invest in HR technology as "a way to become more efficient, to save operating costs, better manage data [and] understand their workforce," says Michael Martin, a New York-based principal with Mercer Human Resource Consulting.

For example, a retail business might be wise to buy a time and attendance application to optimize employee schedules, thereby helping to lower labor costs.

Or companies with contingent labor might consider using a vendor management solution—an application that helps track contract employees such as consultants, temps, and vendor personnel. A company might save money by reducing or boosting its contingent workforce, but it's impossible to know what option saves money unless you have data—such as that generated with vendor management solutions—to back up your decision.

Companies "spend tens of millions of dollars on contingent labor and have no idea what that spend is made up of in terms of skills and talent," says Ed Newman, president of The Newman Group, a Los Angeles-based talent management consulting firm. "Without that insight, when the decision to cut back comes, how do you know where to cut back?"

Recruiting and talent management applications are high priorities during tough times, employers and consultants note. "Usually, the job market changes in a downturn," says Matthew Timberlake, senior systems administrator with the Arizona State Department of Administration, an HR service provider. The state has frozen hiring for all but the most critical positions. While that reduces recruitment, Timberlake says, the talent management system remains vital. "There are fewer open positions; you're getting more applicants," he says. "Selection criteria automation gains importance. You don't want to lose the few good applicants you get for your few postings."

Talent management applications can handle more than just recruiting data. They also may help with skills inventories, succession planning, and identification and development of potential leaders. These functions help with retention during a hiring slowdown or a freeze.

Employers considering a restructuring should take advantage of the workforce planning tools in many talent management applications, Newman says. "Workforce planning tools can give you insights into your workforce and build what-if scenarios," he explains. If economic realities lead to staff reductions, these scenarios can help HR better analyze the possibilities.

Make a Business Case

Tighter budgets mean tougher audiences in the finance department when you request more HR technology dollars, Newman and others say.

Be prepared with a strong business case and data on your expected return on investment (ROI). Focus on functions connected with the business, such as improving the quality of information for decision-making, boosting employee efficiency, and streamlining compliance with regulations.

"You've got to speak the language of the business," says Krey. "Why does it matter? What's the payback? You've got to 'dollarize' the benefit."

For example, when proposing an investment in an onboarding application, don't just talk about "increased productivity" for new employees. Crunch numbers to show how much money that productivity saves.

To justify purchasing a system that automates common HR transactions, measure transaction time or count the steps in the automated process and the time each requires. Compare that with how long the same transactions take on paper. "These are good, solid measures," says Freddye Silverman, a Baltimore-based HR technology consultant with Silver Bullet Solutions.

So-called software-as-a-service is another option for saving money when shopping for HR functions, consultants say. Instead of the traditional delivery model, where companies purchase a license for software installed on the corporate server, software-as-a-service allows users to access the application via the Internet for a monthly subscription fee. Most billing is done on a per-employee or per-user basis, with no upfront implementation costs.

Another possible cost-saver: Buying software services externally via the Internet means HR likely would need less support from internal information technology departments. "Particularly when organizations have reduced staff and tight budgets, IT staff will be pressed into more support" across the company, says Karen Piercy, a Philadelphia-based principal at Mercer.

Software-as-a-service isn't always cheaper than buying a software license, Silverman cautions. "You're never finished paying" for software you can never own, she says. Still, this delivery model may provide needed HR help for an interim period at lower cost.

When shopping for technology in tight times, don't let cost cutting overshadow needs. Function must meet business requirements, Martin says. "A vendor may have something really cheap, but trying to fit your business into it is not the answer. Make sure [the product] fits before looking at price."

Unearth Unused Help

If tough times mean a complete freeze in the HR technology budget, take the opportunity for reassessment. "Stabilize the environment," Cornetto says. "Make sure you're up-to-date and can survive a several-year hiatus from being able to do new things with your technology."

Find functions your HR systems already can do that you simply aren't using. "Often, a system is designed in the first 12 weeks and never revisited," says Robert Mellwig, SPHR, vice president of HR for Destination Hotels & Resorts, based in Englewood, Colorado. "People are just using the tip of the iceberg."

For example, Mellwig notes that modules in Oracle HR can track details such as Form I-9 expirations and performance review dates. These functions aren't always set up in a basic installation, he says. "Turning on" functions like these in an existing system can increase HR's productivity for free.

Some existing systems can be re-purposed to meet challenges. For example, onboarding systems automate transactions related to new employees, from selecting benefits and tax reporting forms to setting up telephone numbers and computer passwords. What these systems do, they also might help undo when a company shrinks. Onboarding solutions "may come in handy on the 'off-boarding' side if we see organizations having to do reductions in force," says Jim Holincheck, managing vice president of Gartner, an IT consulting company based in Stamford, Connecticut.

If you already have an automated onboarding system, examine whether internal IT staff or the vendor could adapt it to handle severance transactions. The tweaks may take work, but the efficiency gained may justify it.

A technology audit—a comprehensive look at your current HR systems—is another good use of time when purchases aren't on the horizon. An audit "looks at all the systems you're using, how you're using the data and how aligned the processes are, what changes are needed within the current system and where you need to go in the future," Piercy says.

Try to have an objective third party, such as a consultant, conduct the technology audit—although internal audits can be successful, and free, if you have the staff to do them. "You want someone who has some independence to some extent," Holincheck says. "Someone from a different part of the organization, not someone with a vested interest" in HR technology.

Talk to Users, Vendors

Look for ways to boost efficiency without investing in hardware, software or consulting fees. Fostering communication among users, tech support, and training staff is a start.

In Timberlake's department, HR technology and management staff use their systems' reporting capabilities to identify functions that are rarely used or that produce time-wasting errors. "We have a feedback loop from customer service to the functional subject-matter experts to training," says Timberlake. "We identify where [the problems] are and focus our training efforts on those areas to make sure the applications are being used well."

An economic downturn may also be time to deepen relations with current vendors. Start by asking vendors about upgrade schedules for your current software; consultants say vendors don't always publicize upgrades.

At Destination Hotels & Resorts, HR management discovered free upgrades available from its talent management vendor. "There were no costs, and the benefits in terms of new functionality and reporting helped to meet our business needs," Mellwig says.

When vendors bring on fewer new customers, you should have better access to their customer support platforms, Mellwig says. "Consider how you might use those services more proactively. Some [vendors will] proactively diagnose your systems for you and give you input on how to maximize your system—you might just need to ask."

If fewer employers invest in HR technology, vendors may be willing to negotiate longer-term contracts or waive some fees. This strategy worked for Mellwig: "We negotiated a one-year extension with our e-recruitment vendor, which would have been more difficult to do in prior years," he says. "We were able to mitigate our renewal costs and maintain flexibility in longer-term pricing options."

Planning Reaps Rewards

Experts stress that all these tactics—linking HR technology to the business, compiling ROI data, looking for efficiencies—should always be part of HR's technology strategy. "Companies that have made their systems work efficiently will do better than others because they did it when they weren't in pain," says Silverman.

Keep HR technology in the spotlight, Timberlake notes, even if you can't invest. "Spend smarter," he says. "Any organization that takes its eye off of technology when things are tight is going to find itself behind the times when things are good again. You need technology vision to be part of your organization's business plan."

"It takes a lot of guts to continue through and make the investment," says Holincheck.

At Capital One, HR's long-term technology focus has helped prepare it for today's smaller budgets. Krey's organization has long followed a structured technology planning process, monitoring systems for usability and business impact, and setting priorities for spending.

"In 2003, we set our short-term and long-term plans, and we're reaping the benefits," Krey says. Capital One sets priorities for HR technology needs based on projected cost savings, productivity gains, and usability. "If more money became available tomorrow, I can tell you what we'd get started on," he says. His advice to other HR professionals: "The best time to start is today."

13 Soft Real Estate Market Impacts Corporate Relocation Programs

Stephen Miller

Facing a softening real estate market, mounting competitive pressures, and a tightening economy, today's corporate relocation managers are modifying their policies to better contain costs and keep employees mobile, according to the second annual survey of relocation policies and practices by Weichert Relocation Resources Inc. (WRRI).[1]

WRRI surveyed corporate relocation and HR professionals from 204 North American employers.

Echoing the results of 2007's survey, rising inventory costs was cited as having the greatest impact on corporate relocation, followed by increases in requests for exceptions to policy and reluctance to relocate.

Among the key findings:

- The soft market is giving rise to duplicate housing costs, with 62 percent of companies covering payments for employees who fail to sell their departure-area homes before moving into their destination-area homes.

- The use of incentives to generate demand and stimulate sales is on the rise to both brokers (28 percent in 2008 over 24 percent in 2007) and buyers (27 percent over 16 percent).

BVO Option: Longer Wait for Sale

Companies hoping to ride out the market slowdown should rethink their devotion to the "buyer value option" (BVO) program, a fixture of many corporate relocation policies, the survey also found.

With BVOs, the employer does not guarantee that it will buy employees' homes. Instead, the program mandates that employees market the property until a buyer is found; this means employees take on the risk that a home may remain on the market for several months.

The survey found that seventy-eight percent of companies that offer a BVO reported experiencing an increase in days on market, the average being 130 days.

"Some companies are reluctant to embrace innovation, sticking with programs and formulas that originated and thrived under more vigorous markets because it's what their peers are doing," says Ellie Sullivan, director of WRRI's Consulting Services group. "While the BVO was certainly an effective tool in years past, under today's market conditions, it's giving rise to policy exceptions, extended temporary living, and duplicate housing costs."

Other noteworthy survey findings include:

- More companies are enforcing selection of pre-screened brokers (up to 65 percent in 2008 from 61 percent in 2007), minimum marketing periods (up to 85 percent from 70 percent), and list-price guidelines (68 percent over 62 percent), in an effort to fortify their employees' sales and marketing efforts.
- A quarter of companies are seeking alternatives to the traditional appraisal process, eliminating costly appeals, and matching employees with pre-selected appraisers.

"These survey findings are consistent with our recent consulting engagements, which show that the single most important strategy for controlling overall relocation program costs is creating demand for employee homes," says Sullivan. "Companies that challenge conventional thinking and identify innovative ways to create this demand will ultimately enjoy lower costs and reduced inventories."

14 Personalized Transition:
Workers Are Demanding More Sophisticated Outplacement Services

Donna M. Owens

The recent rash of layoffs at U.S. companies is putting renewed emphasis on outplacement services. For some workers, the announcements spark painful memories. Damian Birkel still remembers that December day in 1990 when he lost his marketing and merchandising job at a major corporation. It happened on his birthday.

"We [employees] were called together and told we were being let go," recalls Birkel, a mid-level manager at the time. "Dozens of people were basically out on the street."

While the company provided outplacement services to ease the transition, Birkel says the myriad financial, professional, and emotional challenges that accompanied his loss weren't adequately addressed.

While Birkel eventually landed a new position, he vowed "never to forget what it was like to be unemployed.

"People who have lost jobs are most concerned about how they're going to survive," says Birkel, now a career counselor and founder of Professionals in Transition, a North Carolina-based support group for displaced workers. "After the trauma, they need to feel as if someone cares."

The concept of greater "care" and responsibility for workers caught in the cross hairs of cutbacks, downsizings, mergers, acquisitions, and restructurings may be driving some trends in the $3 billion outplacement services industry. Many industry experts say the demand for outplacement services is growing among large and small enterprises alike and across sectors. According to the federal Bureau of Labor Statistics, the total number of mass layoffs—involving at least 50 persons from a single employer—was 15,493 in

2007, up from 13,998 in 2006.

Leading outplacement services providers say new models for helping displaced workers share the following characteristics:

- A move toward equal partnerships between former employees and employers.
- Socially responsible and compassionate behavior.
- Greater choices when it comes to outplacement delivery methods, including increased use of technology.

There is more emphasis on personalized one-on-one career guidance, access to tools to develop employees' critical skills, and special content matched to careers. Experts say employees also want to quickly connect with outplacement services and to maintain those ties until they've achieved their goals.

The Evolution of Outplacement

Employers have been providing outplacement services to employees in transition since the late 1960s. The roots harken back to World War II, when employment services aided returning veterans.

Fast-forward to the 21st century, and outplacement services still remain critical for organizations planning and executing reorganizations and the like.

According to U.S. Department of Labor statistics, some 7.2 million Americans were unemployed as of November 2007, a slight increase over 2006.

Against this backdrop, experts say the changing needs of organizations and their workers are creating an evolution in outplacement services.

"Our firm has moved away from some of what we did 10 years ago," says Jim Appleby, senior vice president of business development with Lee Hecht Harrison, a global career management services company. "Two- or three-day workshops used to be common," explains Appleby, who is based in Charlotte, North Carolina. "Clients were given hard copies of materials and manuals. We would teach them about the job search, resume building, networking, interviewing skills, and negotiating the offer. ... It was almost an information dump."

Today's improved delivery methods may incorporate some of those essentials, Appleby notes, but they avoid a one-size fits-all approach.

"People want more choices and opportunities," he says, adding that Lee Hecht Harrison's outplacement services still incorporate one-on-one counseling, but virtual tools and e-learning, workshops, and teleconferences have been added to meet the learning styles of the different clients the firm serves.

Today's career coaches have wide-reaching backgrounds and knowledge of various industries, Appleby says. They "become more like strategists, especially in the first weeks and months of [a client's] job search."

Tailoring Options

Appleby says the need for increased outplacement services has much to do with shifting workplace demographics.

"For the first time, we have three or four distinct generations in the workplace: Generations X and Y, mid-career workers, and baby boomers," he says. "They're all operating under different cycles of career transition activity. … These transitions all have to be taken into account."

For instance, Lee Hecht Harrison has a program for midcareer workers and baby boomers called, "What's Next? A Roadmap for Exploring the Rest of Your Life." The program is designed to offer options and alternatives to those ages 50 and older by addressing their individual needs.

"We help them determine what is possible," says Appleby. "Some may want to retire, work part time, or do volunteer work. Some may want to do something entrepreneurial and hang out their own shingles. We give them resources that can help."

Tailoring services to separated employees in areas that matter most to them has resonated with leading outplacement services providers nationwide.

Right Management, the world's largest outplacement firm and a subsidiary of international employment giant Manpower Inc., worked with International Communications Research in Media, Pennsylvania, in 2006 to help determine criteria defining satisfaction and success for outplacement candidates.[1]

Researchers polled 21,000 outplacement candidates in 19 countries. Those surveyed were mostly male (59 percent), ages 40 to 49 (39 percent), with salaries from $50,000 to $125,000 (62 percent).

The company learned that employers and employees alike wanted more choices, connections, and measurable results. It learned that displaced employees aren't necessarily just seeking jobs like their previous ones; they more frequently change career directions and seek assistance with changing job functions and industries, and explore a range of work/life options and entrepreneurial and retirement alternatives.

The research showed that forty-two percent of outplacement candidates found new positions through networking, vs. only eight percent who answered an advertisement. This information proved critical in helping the company launch a global outplacement service known as RightChoice.

"It focuses on personalized choice for all candidates—for instance, how they engage in our services, [whether] from home, office, or a combination," says Right Management's Tony Santora, senior vice president and global practice leader for transition services, who is based in Philadelphia.

RightChoice has recently been enhanced with iView, a career development solution that combines web-based technology with one-on-one coaching to help users practice and assess interviewing and presentation skills. With iView, employees respond to preselected custom questions and record answers via webcam. Career counselors then provide guidance and targeted developmental coaching based on individual needs.

Outplacement candidates "can see and hear themselves, then assess their body language and the way they responded to questions," explains Santora.

Structured Support

While workforce reductions may never touch some companies, they have become a painful reality for others across the country.

Novell, a Massachusetts-based software company specializing in network operating systems, numbers among those dealing with the issue.

John Flinders, director of human resources, has been with Novell for about 15 years and says his team has been "a huge supporter" of outplacement services.

"Severance is important, but fairly common," Flinders says. "In addition to cash and money, we're looking to help our people, who have great talent, find other jobs."

The organization contracts with two leading outplacement services firms, including one geared to upper-level executives.

"Some people want to do it on their own, but we strongly encourage them to go to outplacement," says Flinders. "We have people who have not [created] resumes in years; others need [help with] interviewing skills. This allows them to take some responsibility for their careers. ... Ninety-nine percent say they like having someplace to go and something positive to focus on."

In the past, outplacement services typically ended before many candidates achieved their goals. Experts say today's employees in transition are demanding increased accountability, meaning they want to remain continuously connected until the outcomes are successful.

"We get reports about the effectiveness of the services," says Flinders. "That helps us determine the value, and if it's working."

Employees in the banking industry have also been affected by corporate changes. Wachovia Corp., based in Charlotte, North Carolina, announced plans in 2007 to buy A.G. Edwards Inc. in St. Louis. The $6.9 billion merger will reportedly create the second-largest retail brokerage in the nation and displace some employees.

Mark Cupples, Wachovia's HR communications manager, says the company takes its commitment to displaced workers seriously and works with a provider of career transition services to complement its own outreach.

"The first thing we do is set up an on-site career center in the [employees'] locations," says Meredith McGough, a senior vice president and head of recruiting integration. Staffed by a vendor and outfitted with phones and computers, the centers allow employees in transition to meet with career counselors, complete online job searches, refine their resumes, and more. These centers remain operational "as needed," says Cupples.

Providing on-site support can be valuable to employees: Right Management's research found that some eighty-six percent of displaced workers remain in their communities after they've left an organization.

McGough says Wachovia also assigns each transitioning employee a "candidate advocate." Internal advocates help former employees navigate services and sourcing opportunities. With a goal of redeploying talent within the organization wherever possible, advocates possess skills appropriate to those they try to help. For instance, an advocate assigned to a technology worker knows and understands the industry and its needs.

In addition, an HR person "reaches out directly to every employee through personal phone calls and other contact," McGough says.

Wachovia also trains its managers in how to deal with transitioning workers.

"There's a high value placed on preparation of the manager," says Cupples, who notes that all managers must take a required training course called "Displacement Notification Manager Training."

"When we meet with employees to deliver a displacement notification, it is always done in a very private setting, in a caring way," Cupples explains. "We make sure that resources are available on-site or nearby on the day of announcement for employees who may need some space to think through the news. In some instances, we have scheduled conference rooms where EAP [employee assistance program] counselors are available to talk with employees on the day of announcement if needed."

15 Easing the Burden of Financial Stress in the Workplace

Elizabeth Agnvall

In April 2008, Maritz Inc. made a deal with their local Sam's Club to give workers at the sales and marketing services company's headquarters in Fenton, Missouri, a $10 discount on membership. Con McGrath, vice president for people and organizational development said two-thirds of the company's 3,300 employees are based in Fenton, and those workers are feeling the pinch of the high gas prices.

"Most of these folks, virtually all, are getting to work by car. Mass transit is not an option. Most everybody is being impacted by the higher gas prices. It's hurting people in the pocketbook." McGrath said gas prices are generally a dime a gallon cheaper at Sam's Club, and the retailer has discounted prices on food, which helps combat rising grocery bills.

McGrath said the company has seen a slight increase in employees who call the company's employee assistance plan (EAP) for financial assistance such as debt counseling services. He says his company hasn't seen a rise in absenteeism or reduced productivity, but that may be attributable in part to recent changes in company policy.

McGrath said Maritz enhanced its 401(k) plan in 2007 to increase the amount it matches, changed the benefits provider and increased the quality and accessibility of financial education. The company expanded commuter benefits and offers an on-site wellness program with exercise classes to help combat stress.

Maritz is one of an increasing number of employers reaching out to help workers handle financial stress brought on by higher gas and food prices, and mortgage challenges. Experts familiar with financial stress on employees say too much financial burden can lead to increased absenteeism, sick leave, and even alcohol and drug abuse. The spillover costs of too much financial stress in a household can range from excessive time spent on personal phone calls at work to serious psychological problems requiring counseling.

Recent research has found that as gas prices climb, employee productivity can plummet.[1] According to a 2008 survey of 800 full-time employees with an average round trip commute of 30 miles a day, rising gas prices have caused:

- 52 percent to reconsider taking vacations or other recreational activities.
- 45 percent "to fall behind financially."
- 42 percent to cut back on debt-reduction payments, such as credit card payments.
- 39 percent to agree that "Gas prices have decreased my standard of living."
- About a third of respondents to say they would quit their job for a commute nearer to home.
- Nearly 30 percent to consider the consequences of going without basics, including food, clothing, and medicine.

Wayne A. Hochwarter, the Jim Moran Professor of Management at Florida State University's College of Business, who conducted the research, said the employees he surveyed were so concerned with the price of gas that they were less attentive on the job, less excited about going to work, and less passionate and conscientious about their workload. He found little difference in results among people of different occupations, gender, and work tenure.

"What we're finding is that when people are struggling, it's extended beyond the gas prices to just everything, including food and electricity. It gets in their brains and they spend far more time thinking [at work] about how to make ends meet," Hochwarter said.

Signs of Financial Stress

Edward Charlesworth, co-author of *Mind Over Money and Stress Management: A Comprehensive Guide to Wellness*,[2] and the director of Willowbrook Psychological Associates in Houston, said the number one stressor in the United States is money. He said a change in personality or routine is often one of the first signs that some kind of stress—financial or otherwise—is spilling into the workplace.

For example, a person who is typically outgoing might become more withdrawn. An employee might have a drop in performance and an increase in absenteeism. He said he's seen an increase in substance abuse, including alcoholism, brought on by financial pressure.

Oliver Williams, administrative director with the Chicago-based EAP firm Bensinger, DuPont and Associates, said calls around the country regarding financial issues are hovering around eighteen percent, which is about average. He said the company has seen an increase in employees calling with issues surrounding a mortgage problem.

Williams, who has worked as an EAP professional for 25 years, says cyclical changes in the economy over the years often result in anxiety at work. Employees might undergo anxiety, depression, substance abuse, and even domestic violence. Managers might also notice low productivity, inability to focus, and difficult relations with co-workers.

"That's why we want to take the time to talk with the person to see how the financial situation is impacting their lives," Williams said.

Williams said employees who are struggling to make ends meet might take more than the usual amount of personal calls at work or even have wage assignments [garnishment] from debtors.

"A lot of times, HR has to have a bigger eye on work performance issues as they come up. If the performance problem is related to a person's financial condition, that's one indicator that an employee might need help."

Marina London, a spokesperson for the Employee Assistance Professionals Association (EAPA), said employees undergoing financial stress may be irritable, less tolerant of assignments and pressures, and not focused on work. Employees might also ask for advances on their salaries or extra shifts. Although most want concrete help rather than emotional support, she said counseling is extremely valuable if financial woes at home are spilling over into the workplace.

"I don't want to discount the importance of having concurrent supportive counseling," said London, who worked as an EAP executive for large employee assistance programs before joining EAPA. "The concrete financial services are important. It's also important to have an objective ear where you can talk about how stressed you are about what's going on."

More Employers Help

Employers don't typically get involved in employee's financial woes, Hochwarter added, but he's seeing a shift in that attitude. Since he posted his research, he has fielded several calls from companies asking how they can help their employees.

Companies are responding with a variety of methods aimed at reducing the effects of financial stress. The Society for Human Resource Management (SHRM) surveyed its members on this issue in May 2008 and found that gas-cost related assistance rose dramatically over 2007, with forty-two percent of employers raising mileage reimbursement to the IRS cap.[3] The survey found twelve percent of companies help organize carpools, fourteen percent offer public transportation discounts, and fourteen percent reward employee performance with a gas card.

"What's important is for organizations to reach out and find a way to demonstrate some level of concern, some level of care, empathy, and understanding," Hochwarter said.

Long-Term Effects

Some of the changes employers and employees are making because of gas prices and the mortgage crisis might actually benefit society in the long run, according to Charlesworth.

"Our American addictions include money and spending," Charlesworth said. "We've worked ourselves into a corner here, but I think we can heighten our awareness and consciousness."

He said counseling can help change dysfunctional habits and teach people to stop tying their self-esteem to having a Montblanc pen or the latest SUV.

"I think in some ways this is going to be beneficial to start to value ecologically responsible behavior," Charlesworth said. "If you raise the consciousness and start to put the emphasis back to where it should be, then we get back to finding out what really makes us happy anyway."

16 Easing the Burden of Employees' Debt

Peter Weaver and Gina Rollins

At Enterprise Integration Inc., a Jacksonville, Florida-based information technology company, "Some of our people [are] so deep in credit card debt, they can't dig themselves out," says Human Resource Director Kimberly Steigelman, SPHR.

"Some workers have gotten themselves into variable-rate mortgages because they seemed to be a good bet at the time," Steigelman continues. Now, "rates have gone way up, and all too many homeowners can't make their mortgage payments on top of all their other expenses."

It's not just homeowners who have budget problems. "Our employees are struggling with the rising cost of health care and, at the same time, are trying to put away money in 401(k) and other retirement plans," adds Patricia Knight, PHR, an HR manager with Kaplan Early Learning Co. in Lewisville, North Carolina.

According to Howard S. Dvorkin, founder and chief executive officer of Consolidated Credit Counseling Services (CCCS) in Fort Lauderdale, Florida, and author of *Credit Hell: How to Dig Out of Debt*,[1] it's common "to see employees balancing their checkbooks at work, calling their banks, and calling creditors while they are supposed to be on the job."

On top of this, Dvorkin says, more people are getting "second jobs as waiters and waitresses, working at night and working on weekends to the point where they're too tired and not able to focus well on the work at hand."

As bad news mounts on the economic front, more employers are taking a strong proactive approach to help their employees better manage personal finances. Whether through workshops, courses, online resources, or one-on-one sessions with financial counselors, experts say these investments pay big dividends.

"If it saves HR [the time and energy spent on] one wage garnishment per month, it's worth it," contends Catherine M. Williams, who administers financial literacy programs for Money Management International, a nonprofit credit counseling organization in Chicago.

Equipping workers to deal with the financial challenges of life, the argument goes, gives them confidence and security that carries into their work through increased productivity, job satisfaction, and retention.

"In the same way that we have doctors come in to discuss medical topics like diabetes, this is a focus on financial health," explains Linda Fry, HR specialist with the Pompano Beach, Florida, city government.

Employers are not the only ones interested in raising awareness of personal finance. In January 2008, President George W. Bush established the President's Advisory Council on Financial Literacy, made up of leaders from business, faith, and nonprofit communities. The council will work with the public and private sectors to boost financial education efforts, increase access to financial services, establish measures of national financial literacy, and conduct research on financial knowledge.

Not Just Investment Advice

Many credit unions and other employee organizations offer financial management courses for employers to consider. Such personal finance advice goes far beyond that which is offered in the context of retirement planning.

Employees today find "more financial planning responsibilities they have to take responsibility for because the days of paternalistic management support are gone," says Senior Vice President Arthur Mazor at Fidelity HR Services, based in Marlborough, Massachusetts.

Although Fidelity's financial planners generally provide advice on investments rather than budgeting or debt management, Mazor says, "financial planners and other investment experts are brought in for seminars after working hours." Of course, "It has to be made clear that financial planning advice is not coming from the employer."

Make sure you do background research and that financial advisors have all the necessary education, licenses, and certifications, advises Antoinette Pilzner, a shareholder with Butzel Long in Ann Arbor, Michigan. If the employer holds a person or organization out as a resource, the employer has a general fiduciary responsibility under federal and some state laws to vet that entity. Pilzner says it would probably be a good idea to issue a caveat that the employer doesn't recommend the resource, but just makes it available; employees remain free to use any resource they want.

Diverse Offerings

How can employers find experts effective at conveying personal finance information and hands-on problem-solving skills for employee audiences?

"We are getting word-of-mouth referrals from employees who have gone through programs outside of our organization," says Steigelman. She wants to contract with a third party, such as a credit counselor, to offer workshops on-site. "This is from employees coming to me and raising issues confidentially about having credit card problems or issues in the housing market," she explains. "Right now, our answer is to refer them to our employee assistance provider, but we'd like to offer more education to more people and maybe catch people earlier in whatever financial challenges they may be facing."

Stephen Cullum, HR manager for Ampacet Corp., a Tarrytown, New York, manufacturer of colors and additives for the plastics industry, says employees can seek financial advice through either the company's employee assistance provider or its credit union.

However, to expand the financial education available to its workforce, Ampacet plans to pilot a program in 2008 with its 401(k) provider, Wachovia. Representatives from Wachovia will offer financial seminars at Ampacet headquarters. Eventually, the program will be offered to Ampacet employees nationwide. Although many sessions will address investments, several will cover personal finance topics such as budgeting.

Other employers are getting together to provide money management courses for their employees. Five major corporations in Chicago sponsor Money Management International's lunch-and-learn personal finance seminars. A typical three-workshop series costs $125 per person. The sessions focus on financial goal-setting and budgeting; credit issues, including the credit reporting process; and savings. The goal: to build a financial education foundation that enables workers to "move from being spenders to budgeters to savers to investors," says Williams. The number of attendees varies by employer; Williams has presented to audiences ranging from a handful of people at an auto-parts store to groups of 50 at *Fortune* 100 companies.

ComPsych Corp., a Chicago-based provider of employee assistance programs, offers employers lunch-and-learn classes that cover topics such as getting beyond living paycheck to paycheck, teaching children how to manage money, planning and transitioning into retirement, and planning and saving for college.

IBM's MoneySmart program provides in-person and web-based seminars, one-on-one planning sessions, and online tools that cover such issues as managing debt and housing expenditures, budgeting for college, and planning for retirement. Eventually, there will be a protected web portal where employees can maintain personal action lists, store financial data, and access tools and content. Although the $50 million, three-year program, launched in March 2007, coincides with a transition from traditional retirement benefits to a "401(k) Plus Plan," it strives to educate employees about these broader personal finance topics. A year later, 60,000 employees have participated, according to Laurie Friedman, corporate communications spokesperson.

In Pompano Beach, Fry says, "we provide credit counseling for all of our employees." A credit professional from CCCS presents lunch-and-learn programs to make personal finance information available and answer questions about credit and saving. About 20 to 25 people attend each workshop. In four years, 5-7 percent of the city's workforce has made follow-up inquiries to CCCS, according to Fry. The workshops are free to the city; employees who desire one-on-one counseling pay the nonprofit a nominal fee.

All told, Fry says, "these sessions sharpen our employees' sense of well-being and job satisfaction."

According to a recent CCCS survey, American families these days pay more than $1,200 a year in credit card fees and interest, and have an average of $2,500 in unsecured debt in more than two accounts—and their balances keep climbing.

Counseling Helps

As proof of the success of financial education programs, Williams cites the case of a 35-year-old Chicago woman who works for a sales staffing company. The woman has chronic health problems, and her insurance doesn't cover all her expenses. In fact, she missed so much time at work, her paycheck was reduced.

The woman found Money Management International through a list of resources in her employer's HR department. In one-on-one sessions, Williams says, "We helped her work out a budget and put her in touch with resources that could provide access to low-cost medicines." The woman didn't realize she qualified for big discounts. Her employer drew up a schedule where she could work from home two days a week. This cut commuting costs, decreased stress, and ultimately improved productivity.

"Showing employees how to set up a workable budget can be a key to their financial health and productivity," adds Barbara Campbell, director of ComPsych's Financial Connect service, which provides personal finance information and counseling for clients' employees.

"You want a well-educated workforce that manages the wages they're being paid. It lessens HR and payroll issues, and it makes the employees happier and more productive," Williams contends.

17 Employee Forgivable Loans

Anne St. Martin

An "employee forgivable loan" is an employee benefit designed to encourage employees to take a specific action—such as the purchase of a fuel-efficient vehicle or a home in a targeted area, acceptance of a job offer or the pursuit of professional development. The employer determines the maximum amount and terms of the loan, and a portion is forgiven each period (i.e., monthly or yearly), as specified in the employer's policy, until the entire loan is forgiven. The employee is not required to reimburse the employer for the forgiven portion of the loan.

A forgivable loan program should clearly outline what disqualifying events will cause the remaining balance of the loan to become due. The definition of "disqualifying event" can vary based upon the nature of the loan. For example, a disqualifying event for a home purchase loan might be the sale of the home for which the loan was provided. Regardless of the purpose of the loan, employers should consider including separation of employment as a disqualifying event.

A loan is not taxable income to the employee when received. If a loan is repaid, there are no taxable income consequences. However, the Internal Revenue Service (IRS) treats most forgiveness of debt as taxable income. Therefore, the portion of the loan that is forgiven by the employer each period is considered "taxable" income to the employee. The employer is obligated to withhold federal income tax, Social Security, Medicare, and state and local taxes on the amount forgiven as though the employee had received it in his or her gross wages. The amount forgiven should be reflected on the employee's pay stub and included in the annual W-2 Form.

For example, assume eligible employees can receive a forgivable loan of up to $5,000, which can be used to defray down payment, closing costs or points on the purchase of a home in a targeted area. The employer will forgive one-third of the loan each year over a three-year period. Let us say that the employee closes on the purchase of a home in the targeted area on June 1, 2008, and that he or she chooses the full loan amount of $5,000. This date (June 1) will be considered the anniversary date of the forgivable loan. On June 1, 2009, the employer will forgive $1,667 (one-third) of the loan, assuming that the employee fulfills all the conditions of the program. That $1,667 will appear as income to the employee on the W-2 he or she receives from the employer for 2009. It is subject to FICA and all other withholding taxes. The employer will forgive $1,667 on June 1, 2010, and the remaining $1,666 on June 1, 2011. These would appear on the employee's W-2 form for 2010 and 2011, respectively.

Due to the tax consequences, employers should work closely with their legal counsel and payroll departments or vendors to ensure compliance.

18 Keep Workers 401(k)-Focused

Nancy Hatch Woodward

All it took was a two-day snowstorm to get employees centered on their retirement plans.

During the winter of 2008, a Delaware company sponsored a 401(k) education program, a six-hour Saturday session for employees and family members. Because it snowed through the weekend, some participants stayed in on Sunday and did their homework.

One employee and her husband completed every worksheet and exercise their trainer had given them the day before, mapping out their future, including what they should be saving and how they were going to do it, says Susan Windham, chief executive officer of the EDSA Group, a financial education company in Baton Rouge, Louisiana, that conducted the session. The couple "made revisions to their budget and even made a date with their estate planning attorney," she says. "It touched all aspects of their lives."

Although staying indoors during nasty weather may help employees concentrate on retirement plans, a more common motivator can be the stormy economy—buffeted by rising prices, job uncertainties, falling home values, spreading credit woes, roller-coaster stock prices, and the more frequent use of the word "recession." At times like these, employees may grow increasingly uncertain about their retirement prospects, worried that they can't afford to save now for later, tempted to curtail current levels of contributions to 401(k) plans and possibly inclined to tap plans' assets to help make ends meet. And they can be particularly receptive to employer-sponsored education to help them deal with financial concerns.

In fact, providing such information for employees—regardless of the condition of the economy—is an important responsibility that employers take on when they offer employee-directed retirement plans such as 401(k)s.

Employees are indeed worried. According to a 2008 survey from the Transamerica Center for Retirement Studies, employees are losing confidence that their retirement nest eggs will prove sufficient—forty-eight percent of survey respondents said they thought they are saving enough, down from sixty-five percent the previous year.[1]

In addition, loans from 401(k) accounts appear to be on the rise. In the December 2007 Duke University/*CFO Magazine* Global Business Outlook Survey report, nearly twenty percent of companies reported seeing increases in hardship withdrawals from 401(k) accounts. Most of the withdrawals were to prevent home mortgage foreclosures or personal bankruptcies.[2]

According to Transamerica Center, the number of employees who took loans from their retirement plans was up substantially, to eighteen percent from eleven percent the previous year. Almost half of the loans were taken to pay off debt.

Actions Have Consequences

Employees need to realize that withdrawing from a 401(k) account can result in substantial taxes and penalties, says Rick Meigs, president of 401khelpcenter.com, in Portland, Oregon.

Hardship withdrawals from a 401(k) are not for everyone, says Jan Jacobson, senior counsel, retirement policy, at the American Benefits Council, an employer-oriented association specializing in employee benefits, in Washington, D.C. There are strict rules on the granting of hardship distributions, she says.

Jacobson adds that employees should consider how they will pay back loans and whether they will be able to afford to continue contributing to their 401(k) accounts. If they can't continue, they stand to lose their employer's matching contribution.

The potential effects of reducing the value of a 401(k), whether by withdrawing from the account or curtailing contributions to it, are among the core principles of retirement plan management that should be spelled out for employees from time to time, some experts say.

Plan participants should keep in mind, for example, that:

- It's normal for the economy to have ups and downs.

- Recessions are infrequent.
- Investments purchased during a period of decline can rise in value substantially when the economy starts growing again.
- Contributing consistently to a 401(k) can be beneficial in the long term.
- It's important to be diversified in investments and to rebalance a 401(k) account periodically—to alter its mix of higher- and lower-risk components in keeping with the employee's age and nearness to retirement.

Not Tuned In

What concerns benefits expert Dallas Salisbury about employees' management of their 401(k)s is not so much what they do—it's what they don't do. Salisbury is president and CEO of the Employee Benefit Research Institute (EBRI), a private, nonprofit organization in Washington, D.C., that focuses on health, savings, retirement, and economic security issues. "Individuals don't pay attention to what is happening in the world relative to their retirement savings," he says.

Even in a recession, Salisbury notes, employees may stand still. He cites EBRI research that shows 401(k) enrollment, diversification, and contribution rates remained essentially unchanged during the last recession, in 2001, compared with rates in preceding years.

Yet employees could be open to education about 401(k) plans in general. According to EBRI research set forth in The Retirement System in Transition: 2007 Retirement Confidence Survey, more than half of workers indicated that they would be likely to take advantage of professional investment advice offered by the companies that manage their employer-sponsored retirement plans.[3]

"One-third of people say they want investment education from family and friends," says Salisbury. "Employers can't do much about that; however, survey data show that more people will listen to investment information from their employer than a third party"—with "third party" understood to include the company that administers the employer-sponsored plan.

Stacy Henderson, president of KMotion, an employee financial education company in Tualatin, Oregon, suggests that if you do use a third party—whether the administrator of your 401(k) plan or a resource separate from your plan—it's important that HR or someone in senior management be involved as a co-presenter of the session or at least stand up and introduce the presenter. The reason, essentially, is credibility. She says employees are more likely to trust their own managers rather than outsiders with regard to such information. Some employees may be skeptical of a message regarding the management of their 401(k) plans that comes only from someone who may appear to have a stake in employees acting on the message.

Crafting a Careful Message

At all times—and especially during a downturn, when 401(k) balances may be declining—many employers worry about how they provide financial information to employees. There is longstanding concern that if investment education is perceived as advice and, when acted on, produces a negative result, the employer will be held legally liable for that outcome.

Supplying investment advice rather than just education can raise both fiduciary and possibly prohibited-transaction issues, says Christopher G. Guldberg, a partner in the Chicago office of the global law firm Baker & McKenzie LLP. His advice: Relax. Most cases dealing with fiduciary responsibilities involve employer stock, he says.

The rules are pretty simple, Guldberg continues. First, don't endorse any type of investment strategy or product. You can, however, educate employees about:

- The benefits of participating in a 401(k) plan.
- The benefits of increasing contributions to the plan.
- General financial investment concepts such as risk and diversification.
- Asset allocation models, showing examples of, say, investors at different ages who may prefer more-conservative investments or who are interested in taking more risks with their portfolios.
- Questionnaires, worksheets and software in which no recommendations are made but a user can plug in their information and figure out for themselves what investments might be appropriate.

In fact, just the act of filling out a financial plan for retirement can be useful, says Jean Setzfand, director of financial security at AARP in Washington, D.C. A November 2007 AARP report, "Preparation for Retirement: The Haves and Have-Nots," notes that among people who said they had taken time to calculate how much money they will need for retirement, eighty-one percent said that as a result they started saving more, seventy-seven percent paid off all or some debt, fifty-five percent reduced their spending, and fifty-three percent enrolled in a retirement plan at work.[4]

Means and Methods

Seminars can be helpful, but the most effective approach, Setzfand says, is to hold either small-group or one-on-one meetings. They tend to produce the most beneficial changes in investing behavior.

Windham says some employees may be intimidated by the prospect of meeting privately or in a small group with a financial professional because they don't feel they know enough. She suggests that having employees attend a larger seminar or complete an online training session ahead of time can help them prepare for one-on-one or small-group meetings.

Although it can be important during an economic downturn to remind employees about investing concepts such as dollar-cost averaging, asset allocation, and the positive returns of equity investing over the long haul, it's best to sidestep such technical themes at the start when getting employees involved in financial education, says Meigs. Investment jargon can lose an audience quickly.

"Talk about practical things—the employer match, for instance. That resonates with people. They understand that," Meigs says.

Keep in mind that employees burdened with debt or barely scraping by may not be ready to hear about savings because they don't feel they are in a position to take advantage of it, Windham explains. When the presentation turns to why employees are not participating or not increasing their contributions, about forty percent indicate that they don't have the dollars, Meigs says. So it's necessary to educate employees on how they can find the money to put into their retirement savings accounts.

People relate better to examples similar to their own experiences, experts say. Using managers' or co-workers' testimonials about the importance of saving for retirement—and how detrimental it is not to save—makes a strong impact, according to Henderson. In its presentations, the EDSA Group uses fictitious families to represent employees' situations. Participants see the changes the fictitious families need to make to improve their financial situations, Windham says. "Once they see how it works for others, they can apply it to their lives."

Men and women react differently to various features of retirement savings plans, says Punam Keller, the Charles Henry Jones Third Century Professor of Management at the Tuck School of Business at Dartmouth College. In a summary of her research on "the power of social marketing for encouraging employees to participate in savings and wellness programs," she writes that "men's contributions to pension savings plans are not influenced" by plan rules or investment guidance.[5]

On the other hand, she continues, "we believe that even though women are bigger savers than men, they are less likely to contribute when they do not have guidance on how to invest. And they appreciate structure (same amount/same time), flexibility (to withdraw), and ease of implementation (scheduled payments)."

Will It Work?

Retirement planning education won't motivate everyone, of course. Salisbury says the employer must keep in mind that only 25-30 percent of participants will take advantage of the education.

Nonetheless, employers must reach out to those who will take advantage of what's offered, providing tools and information they can use to make sensible financial planning decisions now and to avoid taking actions that may hurt them in the long run. At least, employers can set the tone by emphasizing that the long-term strategies of retirement planning should not be compromised by short-term tactics that could diminish the effectiveness of their 401(k) accounts.

Investing can be an emotional process for employees, says Setzfand. "They think, 'Oh my God, there is a recession on the way, the economy is going down, the market is plummeting. I should do something like take all my money out of the stock market.'" Whether such action would be wise or unwise is the employee's decision, of course, but it can be the employer's responsibility to make sure employees have the information necessary to make the best decisions.

19 The Difference between a Furlough, a Layoff, and a Reduction in Force

The terms *furlough*, *layoff*, and *reduction in force* (RIF) describe actions that are intended to achieve cost savings by reducing a company's payroll costs. Even though the words have been used interchangeably, their true meanings are quite different.

A furlough is considered to be an alternative to layoff. When an employer furloughs its employees, it requires them to work *fewer hours* or to take a certain amount of unpaid time off. For example, an employer may furlough its employees one day a week for the remainder of the year, and pay them for only 32 instead of their normal 40 hours each week. Another method of furlough is to require all employees to take a week or two without pay sometime during the year.

An employer may require all employees to go on furlough, or it may exempt some employees who provide essential services. Generally, though, the theory is to have the majority of employees share some hardship as opposed to a few employees losing their jobs completely. Employers must be careful when furloughing exempt employees, so that they continue to pay them on a salary basis and do not jeopardize their exempt status under the Fair Labor Standards Act (FLSA). A furlough that encompasses a full workweek is one way to accomplish this, since the FLSA states that exempt employees do not have to be paid for any week in which they perform no work.

A layoff is a *temporary* separation from payroll. An employee is laid off because there is not enough work for him to perform; his employer, however, believes that this condition will change and intends to recall him when work again becomes available. Employees generally are able to collect unemployment benefits while laid off without pay, and frequently an employer will allow them to maintain benefits coverage as an incentive to remain available for recall.

Once management has determined that an employee will not be recalled to work, the layoff becomes *permanent* and is more accurately called a reduction in force, or a termination. A RIF involves a permanent cut in head count that also can be accomplished by means of attrition. When an employee is terminated pursuant to a reduction in force, it is sometimes referred to as being "riffed." However, some employers use layoff as a euphemism for what is actually a permanent separation. This may be confusing to the affected employee, allowing him to believe that recall is a possibility, and preventing him from devoting his full energies toward locating a new position.

Having a probationary period can weaken an employer's claim that employment is at-will. Probationary periods are commonly thought of as a specified period during a new employee's first few months in which the employee can be terminated at any time. At-will employment is a common law concept that allows employees and employers to terminate the employment relationship at any time for any reason, except for reasons that are specifically prohibited by law or by contract.

However, some courts have found a problem with employers with probationary periods. The employers imply that while employees can be terminated for any lawful reason during the probationary period, employees are entitled to retain employment after that period unless the employer can show just cause for the termination.

Employers can avoid this implication by removing all references to probationary periods and including at-will disclaimers in employment applications, offer letters, and the employee handbook.

Some employers have a practice or policy of having an "introductory period" or an "orientation period" during which the employee is being trained and is continuing to be assimilated into the organization through formal and informal means. Often, the employee and the supervisor meet to establish performance goals at the end of the orientation period. Employers who use introductory periods need to avoid implying that it will be harder for employees to be terminated after the designated period is over.

It may be possible to use technological means to block these e-mails. This would be an option to explore with the company's IT specialists. Also determine if the employee signed a separation/severance agreement that includes a clause that prohibits disparagement or defamation against the employer. If such a non-disparagement agreement exists, contact the former employee to remind him of this and request that the messages stop immediately. If the former employee continues sending messages, check with your attorney regarding legal remedies.

If there is no signed separation agreement that includes a non-disparagement clause, you still may want to discuss this situation with the corporate legal counsel. The company may be able to file a lawsuit against the former employee for defamation (false or misleading statements that damage reputation).

In a recent court case, an employer facing similar conduct from a former employee filed a lawsuit against the individual citing violation of a type of trespass, called trespass to chattel, which involves damaging but not actually intruding on real property. The initial decision favorable to the employer, however, was overturned by the state supreme court, which cited freedom of speech protection for the former employee.

As with other employee relation situations, employers need to focus on prevention strategies. For example, whenever an involuntary termination occurs and a separation/severance agreement is used, consider including a non-disparagement clause in the agreement.

As with any binding agreement, check with your attorney for definitive guidance.

20 Selecting Employees for Layoff

Once the decision has been made to downsize, what criteria should be used in selecting employees for layoff? In a perfect world, such decisions could be eradicated by ranking all of the jobs within the organization into specific job categories and by eliminating the positions no longer necessary to the continued success of business operations. Unfortunately, this is not a perfect world, and carrying out widespread layoffs can pose greater challenges and risks to employers.

Several options are available when planning dreaded, but sometimes necessary, workforce reductions. It should go without saying, however, that you should carefully plan layoff selection before executing an organizational downsizing to ensure that selection criteria do not result in disparate treatment or have an adverse impact on protected groups. In addition, you should research the federal Equal Employment Opportunity Commission (EEOC) and the state fair employment practice laws to minimize inherent risks of potential discriminatory charges.

Although it is virtually impossible for any employer to ever truly obtain risk-free status in implementing workforce reductions, carefully planned and executed downsizing plans used in conjunction with good documentation and layoff policies (which have been reviewed by legal counsel) can be an employer's strongest defense against allegations of discrimination. Employers in unionized environments need to take additional precautions to ensure that an existing collective bargaining agreement is not violated.

Selection for Downsizing

Seniority-Based Selection

With seniority-based selection, the "last hired/first fired" concept is used. Because seniority-based systems reward employees for their tenure, there is a lower risk that older workers will sue employers for age discrimination under the Age Discrimination in Employment Act (ADEA). However, using seniority does not protect the employer from further risks for potential discrimination against other protected groups.

Employee Status-Based Selection

Employers who have part-time or contingent workers on their payrolls may want to lay off those workers first to ensure greater job security for remaining core workers. Unless an employer's workforce is made up largely of contingent workers, this method alone may not be sufficient to meet downsizing needs, and it may need to be used in conjunction with other selection criteria.

Merit-Based Selection

Although this method of selection is often a preferred choice among many managers because of its added flexibility for weeding out marginal or poorly performing employees, it should be scrutinized carefully. Because merit selection criteria are based either in part or in whole on performance evaluation information (which is not always objective and may contain rater biases), this method has not been proven to provide an accurate qualitative means for ranking the differences among individual employees' performance in selecting employees for layoff.

Skills-Based Selection

With this type of system, it is sometimes possible for employers to retain those workers who have the most sought-after skills. However, be aware that this method may cause a company to retain younger workers with needed and versatile skill sets, and to lay off older workers who may not have the necessary skills. The older workers are protected from discrimination by the ADEA.

Multiple Criteria Ranking

Although all of the above methods can be equally effective when planned carefully, it has been argued that perhaps the most effective method of selection is using a combination of all the criteria previously discussed.

Below is a sample of the ranking criteria used by some organizations that have implemented selection policies that are based on multiple criteria such as seniority, skill, and performance considerations.

- Employee's promotability and attitude
- Employee's skills, abilities, knowledge, and versatility
- Employee's education and experience levels
- Employee's quantity and quality of work
- Employee's attendance history
- Employee's tenure within the company

The Tools:
Definitions, Guidelines, Sample
Policies, Letters, and Forms

21 WARN Notice*

Notice of Layoff to Affected Employees Pursuant to the Worker Adjustment and Retraining Notification (WARN) Act

To:_____   _____
           Name of Employee   Position

Date:_____

As has been previously announced, ABC Company will experience a reduction in its workforce, and a number of employees of ABC Company will experience layoffs, as a result of a significant downturn in business and corporate-wide reorganization. This notice, which is issued in compliance with the Worker Adjustment and Retraining Notification (WARN) Act, is to inform you that you are likely to be laid off due to the loss of business revenue and related reorganization. The purpose of this notice is to provide you with the answers to some questions that you may have regarding your layoff so that you can prepare to locate other employment. The information provided below represents the best information available to the company at the time this notice was issued.

* *This sample courtesy of the Law Firm of Ray & Isler, Vienna, Virginia.*

Is my layoff going to be permanent or can I expect to be recalled to employment at some time in the future?

At this time, you should consider your layoff permanent. As part of the corporate reorganization, ABC Company will attempt to continue operation of its manufacturing facilities by obtaining additional contracts or new business. If these efforts are successful, some employees may be maintained or recalled to work. However, because the success of such efforts are entirely unknown at this time, no ABC Company employee who is being laid off should count on being recalled to employment with the company.

When will the layoffs begin and when am I likely to be laid off?

ABC Company expects layoffs to begin around _____. The layoffs may come in stages, depending upon the need for workers as the joint venture moves towards dissolution. Your employment is likely to end around_____, but your layoff may be sooner or later, again depending upon the business need to maintain workers as the full impact of the business downturn and the resulting corporate reorganization becomes known.

Do I have any right to "bump" other employees from their jobs based on my seniority with the company?

ABC Company does not recognize strict seniority rights, but may take seniority into consideration as a factor in determining which employees to layoff and the timing of each employee's layoff. Seniority also will be considered as a factor in recalling employees, should ABC Company be successful in maintaining operation of the facilities. However, seniority will be just one factor in these decisions, and other factors, such as business necessity, expertise, and past performance, also will be taken into account in making these decisions.

Will the company be providing any severance benefits to employees who are laid off?

The company has established a Reduction in Force Policy and a Severance Pay Plan to provide employees with further information regarding their employee benefits and to assist employees during this difficult time. If you have not received a copy of either the Reduction in Force Policy or the Severance Pay Plan summary plan description, you may obtain copies by contacting _____at (   ) _____ – _____ .

Whom can I contact for further information?

If you have further questions or need additional information, you may contact _____ at (   ) _____ – _____ .

22

Older Workers Act Waiver*

Waiver of Claims under the Age Discrimination in Employment Act

The Employee recognizes that, in signing this Release of Claims, Employee is waiving Employee's right to pursue any and all claims under the Age Discrimination in Employment Act, 29 U.S.C. § 626 et seq. (ADEA) arising prior to the date that Employee executes this Release. The Employee understands that Employee may take twenty-one (21) days from the date this Release is presented to Employee to consider whether to execute this Release. The Employee is advised that Employee may wish to consult with an attorney prior to execution of this Release. Once Employee has executed this Release, Employee may revoke the Release at any time during the seven (7) day period following the execution of the Release. After seven (7) days have passed following the Employee's execution of this Release, the execution of this Release shall be final and irrevocable.

* This sample courtesy of the Law Firm of Ray & Isler, Vienna, Virginia.

23 Letter of Transfer

Dear (name):

This letter is to confirm your [contractual/lateral] transfer to the position of (class title) with (organization/department name), effective (date).

Your salary upon transfer will be $ per hour/or annual. You will [not be required to serve a probationary period / be placed on a ( )-month permissive probationary period, which may be shortened at the discretion of your supervisor].

[Select appropriate language from A, B, C, or D.]

Nonrepresented

A. Exempt
Your new position is not included in a certified bargaining unit and it is exempt under the Fair Labor Standards Act provision for overtime.

B. Nonexempt
Your new position is not included in a certified bargaining unit and it is non-exempt under the Fair Labor Standards Act provision for overtime. Should your supervisor assign overtime hours, you will be paid at a premium rate or shall be credited with compensatory time off at a rate of 1.5 hours per hour worked, for all hours worked in excess of 40 hours in a work week. At

the discretion of the employer, compensatory time credits may be provided as payment for overtime. Such compensatory time credits received may be preserved, used or cashed out at the discretion of the employer.

Represented

C. Exempt

Your new position is included in the (identify bargaining unit) bargaining unit and it is exempt under the Fair Labor Standards Act provision for overtime.

D. Nonexempt

Your new position is included in the (identify bargaining unit) bargaining unit and it is nonexempt under the Fair Labor Standards Act provision for overtime. Should your supervisor assign overtime hours, you will be paid at a premium rate or shall be credited with compensatory time off at a rate of 1.5 hours per hour worked, for all hours worked in excess of 40 hours in a work week. At the discretion of the employer, compensatory time credits may be provided as payment for overtime. Such compensatory time credits received may be preserved, used or cashed out at the discretion of the employer.

Please report to me (or supervisor's name) on (date) at (time) to review your new duties and responsibilities. We trust your assignment with us will prove to be both challenging and rewarding.

It is the policy of (name of unit/dept) to provide reasonable accommodation for qualified employees with disabilities. If you need accommodation to perform the essential functions of your position, please contact Human Resources at (999) 999-9999.

Sincerely,
(Supervisor/Chair)

24 Transportation Benefit Plan Enrollment/Change/Cancellation Form

This form authorizes automatic payroll deductions on a pretax basis for qualified transportation expenses under the company's Transportation Benefit Plan (TBP) and in compliance with IRS Code Section 132(f). It may also be used to authorize a change or cancellation of participation in the plan. If you would like to enroll in the program, make a change or cancel your current enrollment, please complete this form and submit it to Human Resources at least 10 business days prior to the 1st of the month for an effective date of the 1st of the next month.

Employee name: _____

Social Security number: _____

Department: _____

For initial enrollment, please complete the following:

❏ Mass Transit (Maximum $115 per month effective 01/01/08) $ _____ per month
Mass transit includes bus, subway, train and ferry for personal use when commuting to work. Receipts or cancelled checks must be attached.

❏ Van Pool (Maximum $115 per month effective 01/01/08) $ _____ per month
Van pools must be used from the employee's place of residence to the place of employment and must be able to seat six passengers, not including the driver. Receipts or cancelled checks must be submitted.

❏ Parking (Maximum $220 per month effective 01/01/08) $$ _____
per month
Parking must be in a lot at or near our location or parking at a location from which the employee commutes to work, such as a subway station. Receipts or cancelled checks must be attached.

For a change, including a cancellation of participation, please complete the following:
Please change my deduction as follows:

❏ Mass Transit: from current $_____ per month to $ _____ per month
❏ Van Pool: from current $_____ per month to $_____ per month
❏ Parking: from current $ _____ per month to $_____ per month

For cancellation of participation, please complete the following:
Please cancel my deduction as follows:

❏ Mass Transit: current $ _____ per month
❏ Van Pool: current $_____ per month
❏ Parking: current $_____ per month

Employee Signature:_____

Date of Submission: _____

Effective date will be 1st of the month if this form is correctly completed and submitted 10 business days prior to the 1st of the month.

25 Transportation Benefit Plan Reimbursement Request

Employee name: _____

Social Security number: _____

Department: _____

Please complete all information requested and attach copies of receipts or both sides of cancelled checks as evidence of expenses incurred and services received.

Transportation expenses eligible for reimbursement:

- Mass Transit (maximum $115 per month effective 01/01/08): Mass transit includes bus, subway, train and ferry for personal use when commuting to work. Receipts or cancelled checks must be attached.
- Van Pool (maximum $115 per month effective 01/01/08): Van pools must be used from the employee's place of residence to the place of employment and must be able to seat six passengers, not including the driver. Receipts or cancelled checks must be submitted.
- Parking (maximum $220 per month effective 01/01/08): Parking must be in a lot at or near our location or at a location from which the employee commutes to work, such as a subway station. Receipts or cancelled checks must be attached.

	Type of Expense	Date of Service	Service Provider	Amount
1				
2				
3				
TOTAL				

I certify that the above information is correct, and I authorize payment from my transportation benefits account.

Employee Signature:_____

Date of Submission: _____

26 Telecommuting Application

Name: _____ Title: _____

Department: _____ Supervisor: _____

Number of days I would like to telecommute: 2 or 3

Please describe how you think your job responsibilities are suited for telecommuting:

Supervisor

I have discussed the possibility of telecommuting with the above mentioned employee. I believe this employee is a good candidate based on job responsibilities and performance in his or her current position.

Supervisor's Signature: _____ Date: _____

Telecommuting Applicant

I have discussed telecommuting with my supervisor and understand that my application does not guarantee that I will be eligible to telecommute. I have read the telecommuting policy and understand that it is not an entitlement and that it is not appropriate for every employee. I understand that telecommuting can be terminated at any time by [Enter Company Name] or me.

Telecommuting Applicant's Signature:_____

Date:_____

Human Resources

Approval_____ Disapproval _____

Reason:_____

_____

_____

_____

Signature:_____ Date: _____

27 Compressed Workweek

How To Develop a Policy and Policy Outline

A compressed workweek is one in which employees work the same amount of hours in fewer than the customary number of days per week. Commonly this would mean working less than five days in one week or less than 10 days in one pay period. Compressed workweeks are slightly more common during the summer and may be known as "summer hours" schedules.

Possible Benefits of Compressed Workweeks:

- Reduced commuting time for employees (may help meet obligations under the Clean Air Act as well).
- Reduced employee costs for transportation, childcare or other daily work-related expenses.
- Increased morale and possible increases in productivity or customer service as a result of improved morale.

Possible Drawbacks of Compressed Workweeks:

- Lack of supervision during some hours of the workday.
- Potential reductions in productivity or customer service due to longer working hours.
- Increased stress in some occupations from repetitive work or "burnout."

- Periodic absenteeism has a proportionately greater impact on work time.
- Union issues related to work hours, breaks, meal periods, etc., may inhibit such a change.
- State law limitations on number of hours worked per day for overtime purposes and other possible state law constraints on adoption of such a program. (California is one state with very specific requirements for adopting flexible work schedules.)
- Administration of payroll, leave and holidays may be slightly more complicated.

Important Policy Elements:

- Management rights clause: The policy should make it clear that this is an optional benefit that can be discontinued at any time for any reason (though efforts should be made to provide reasonable notice where possible).
- Impact on paid holidays: The policy should not conflict with existing holiday and leave allocation practices but should clearly state what the impact will be on compressed workers if a holiday occurs during a compressed week. There should be equitable treatment so that participants receive the same time off and holiday pay as other workers. Some options include reverting to the regular schedule for any week or pay period in which a holiday is planned, offering an alternative floating holiday for compressed workers already scheduled to be off on a planned holiday, allowing compressed workers to rearrange their schedule during a holiday week to ensure they are appropriately compensated and granted holiday time off, etc.
- Impact on paid leave: Options will vary depending upon whether paid leave is allocated by the hour or by the day and should be consistent with existing paid leave policies and equitable for compressed workers and non-compressed workers.
- Eligibility factors: Will all jobs be eligible for compressed work or will it depend upon scheduling issues, staffing levels, and supervision? The policy should clearly state who is eligible and ensure that the policy is fairly and consistently administered.

Policy Outline

Note: Use this outline as a tool for drafting a compressed workweek policy. Once all issues are addressed, the policy can be reformatted to match other existing policies.

Effective _____ , XYZ Corporation will offer eligible employees the opportunity to apply for permission to work on a compressed workweek schedule. A compressed workweek is one in which employees work the same number of hours as normal but in fewer than five days in one week or fewer than 10 days in one pay period. Compressed work schedules will be granted in situations where job and business-related needs can continue to be met even under a compressed schedule.

This policy is in effect: [choose one]

- For a trial period of X weeks beginning ____ and ending_____
- All year
- Summer Season Only (i.e. Memorial Day to Labor Day)
- Other: _____

This policy is available: [choose one]

- For all employees
- For all employees with_____ months/years of services
- For all employees in _____department
- For exempt employees only
- Other: _____

The compressed workweek schedule used will be [choose one or more, after carefully considering normal working hours, the impact on the pay week and the effect on business operations].

- 4/10—participants work either Monday through Thursday or Tuesday through Friday each week
- 9/8—participants work nine hours each day for eight days, eight hours on a ninth day and then take a tenth day off
- 3/12—participants work three days at 12 or 12 ½ hours each day

- 9/9—participants work nine hours for nine days with the tenth day off
- Eight-day week—participants work 10 hours for eight straight days and have a four-day weekend

Exempt employees, by definition, will continue to receive the same salary from week to week regardless of the schedule worked.

Non-exempt employees may be subject to a one-time pay week adjustment to accommodate the new schedule, in accordance with the Fair Labor Standards Act.

Compressed workers eligible for holidays should [indicate what action is to be taken with regard to taking and recording time off] when a holiday falls on a day they are not scheduled to work and should [indicate what action is to be taken] when a holiday falls on a day they are scheduled to work.

Compressed workers eligible for paid leave should [indicate what action is to be taken with regard to taking and recording time off] when taking paid leave on a day otherwise scheduled as work time.

XYZ Corporation reserves the right to suspend, cancel or amend this policy at any time. We also reserve the right to cancel or suspend use of such a schedule by any employee who experiences performance problems deemed to be related to the new schedule. Such circumstances will be evaluated on a case-by-case basis.

28 Flextime Request Form

Employee Name:_____ Date:_____
Printed

Department: _____ Position:_____

Date of Hire: _____

Description of Flextime Arrangement:

Hour of Arrival: _____

Hour of Departure: _____

Beginning Date for Flextime: _____

I have read and understand the company's Flextime Policy. If this flextime arrangement is suspended or cancelled, I will return to a standard work schedule.

Signature of Employee: _____

Date: _____

Approval of Supervisor: _____
Signature

Name:_____ Date:_____
Printed

Copies: Human Resources, Payroll

29 Flexible Work Arrangement Agreement

This flexible work arrangement agreement is established between [Company Name] and [Employee Name].

This agreement shall become effective as of _____ and shall remain in effect until _____ unless modified or terminated by [Company Name], the employee, or the supervisor or successor to the supervisor of the employee. In the event that either the company or the employee needs to terminate the agreement that party shall provide the other party with four weeks written notice. However, in the event of a workplace emergency, the agreement may be suspended immediately and indefinitely. This agreement may be reviewed at any time if requested by either party.

This agreement is subject to the employee satisfying the following conditions on a continuing basis:

- The employee shall perform all job duties at a satisfactory performance level
- The employee's work schedule does not interfere with normal interactions with his/her supervisor, co-workers, or customers
- The employee's schedule does not adversely affect the ability of other company employees to perform their jobs
- The employee assures his/her accessibility to co-workers who maintain the company's regular working schedule
- The employee's paid leave will be earned and used in the same manner

as prior to this flexible work arrangement agreement and be subject to all other applicable company leave policies

■ The employee maintains this agreed-upon work schedule

All of the employee's obligations and responsibilities, and terms and conditions of employment with the company remain unchanged, except those specifically changed by this agreement. Any non-compliance with this agreement by the employee may result in modification or termination of the flexible work arrangement established by this agreement. Such modification or termination will require four weeks notice to the employee.

Flexible Work Schedule: _____

I have read and understand this agreement and all its provisions. By signing below, I agree to be bound by its terms and conditions.

Employee Signature _____ Date _____

Approved by:
Name of Supervisor _____ Date _____

30 Alternative Work Schedule Policy

[Company Name] is interested in alternative work schedules as a method of staff retention through work/life balance. Alternative scheduling is available to assist employees in meeting their personal work performance goals and family needs. Alternative work scheduling is an opportunity to maintain employee productivity through various forms of creative work scheduling.

All [Company Name] employees will be considered for alternative work scheduling on a case-by-case basis, where creative work schedules have been shown to accomplish both work and personal goals, to provide coverage for individual department operations and to serve the company as a whole with increased productivity at no expense to quality output.

There are various alternative work schedule options available to employees. The options include:

- Flextime, which is a block of time at the start and end of traditional eight-hour shifts during which employees may report and complete their required shift hours of work.
- Ten-hour day, four-day workweek, in which an employee works 10 hours per workday, reducing the workweek to four days a week. Employees would still receive regular holiday pay as outlined in the Holiday Pay Policy. If an employee accepts this option, he or she would forgo overtime unless work is performed outside of the agreed schedule.

- Nine-hour day, one day off every other week, in which an employee works nine-hour workdays and permitting the approved employee to reduce every other workweek to a four-day workweek.

Job-sharing is defined as two part-time employees assigned to the same job equivalent as one full-time employee. The position is shared between the two employees. Job-sharing, as an alternative work schedule, must ensure the continuity of the work being done at the same workstation with two individuals working as a team to accomplish one full-time position's duties.

The department director/manager is responsible for identifying if any of the aforementioned staffing options are workable within his or her department. This includes determining if the entire department or an entire shift must convert to one of the above alternative scheduling options. To determine whether it would be appropriate for volunteers to take on these work schedules, the director/manager must assess the impact and outcome in terms of production, quality, and absenteeism, and if one or a combination of the above is in the best interests of the department, company and employee.

Implementation and the determinations of potential schedules must be approved with the consent of the Human Resources department to assess overall feasibility and trial operations prior to announcement and implementation.

The vice president for Human Resources has the general responsibility of overseeing the day-to-day implementation of this policy in accordance with payroll and legal requirements. Any requests for exceptions to this policy should be made in writing to the Human Resource department for review and approval. Only the vice president, Human Resources, or his/her designee, in consultation with the president and the affected department director/manager, may grant such an exception.

31 Job-Sharing Memo of Understanding

Position To Be Job-Shared: _____

Date Job Share To Commence:_____

Employees participating in Job Share:

Name:_____

Name:_____

Job-Share Agreement

- Both employees will equally share one whole job, including all of its responsibilities and duties. Each employee will be accountable for all job duties and everything related to the job.
- Job-share agreement will be for a six-month trial period, and at the end of this period, employees engaged in the job share and the manager will evaluate the effectiveness of the job share.
- If deemed successful by the manager, the arrangement will be evaluated at least annually. As long as there is sustained success, the agreement will continue as long as both employees are employed in the same job with [Company Name].
- Both employees and the manager are committed to making the job share work and will proactively seek resolutions to problems that may

arise. Either employee or the manager involved in the job share may end the job-share agreement at any time for any reason. This should be communicated to the manager and employees involved in the job-share agreement as soon as possible.

- Both employees will each work three days per week (48 total hours, 24 hours per employee), with Wednesday as the overlapping day of the week. The overlapping day is vital to the success of the job share, and this time should be used to share information and work together to make the rest of the week's job share a success.

- In the event that one of the job-share partners terminates employment, changes jobs within the [Company Name] or requests full-time work, the position will automatically revert to a full-time position with the expectation that the remaining job-share partner will assume the full-time requirements of the above position, including a 40-hour workweek. If a compatible partner could be found and it is agreeable to the employer and both employees, the job share agreement could continue.

Signatures below constitute agreement to the job-share agreement above. Either employee or the manager involved in the job share may end the job-share agreement at any time for any reason.

Employee: _____ Date: _____

Employee: _____ Date: _____

Manager: _____ Date: _____

Human Resources: _____ Date: _____

32 Summer Flextime Policy

The operating days and hours of [Name of Company] are Monday through Friday, 8:30 a.m. to 5 p.m. All employees are expected to be at work during these hours. Flexible work schedules are not permitted, except during the summer months, starting the week in which Memorial Day is observed and ending the week in which Labor Day is observed.

The summer flextime at [Name of Company] is a work schedule that allows employees to work extra time on an alternating workweek basis Monday through Thursday in order to leave at 1 p.m. on Friday. The time of arrival and departure may not differ from the standard operating hours by more than two hours, except for the Friday early departure. For example, a typical summer flextime arrangement is Monday through Thursday arriving at 8:30 a.m. and departing at 6 p.m., and on Friday arriving at 8:30 a.m. and departing at 1 p.m.

Supervisors approve flextime on a case-by-case basis. The employee must first discuss possible summer flextime arrangements with his or her supervisor and then submit a written request using the Summer Flextime Request Form. The supervisor will approve or deny the flextime request based on staffing needs, the employee's job duties, the employee's work record and the employee's ability to temporarily or permanently return to a standard work schedule when needed.

A summer flextime arrangement may be suspended or cancelled at any time. Exempt employees must depart from any flextime schedule to perform their jobs. Nonexempt employees may be asked to work overtime, regardless of a flextime schedule.

33 Summer Flextime Request Form

Employee Name:_____ Date:_____

Printed

Department: _____ Position:_____

Description of Summer Flextime Arrangement:

Hour of Arrival: _____

Hour of Departure: _____

Beginning Date for Flextime: _____

(Must be between week in which Memorial Day is observed and week in which Labor Day is observed. Summer flextime is permitted to be taken by an employee on alternating workweeks so that the office is adequately staffed.)

I have read and understand the Company's Summer Flextime Policy. If this flextime arrangement is suspended or cancelled, I will return to a standard work schedule.

Signature of Employee: _____

Date: _____

Approval of Supervisor: _____

Signature

Name:_____ Date:_____

Printed

34 Take the Summer Off Program Policy

Employees may request to be considered for the Take the Summer Off Program. Approval to participate is at management's discretion, based on the impact of the requested absence on operations.

Under the program, eligible employees will be permitted to take a leave of absence without pay for four to 12 weeks during the summer. Periods of leave must be a minimum of four weeks and must begin and end in accordance with [Company Name] pay periods. There are no exceptions to this rule.

All interested employees must have completed probation before June 1 of the year in which they request to participate in the program. The leave requested must begin no earlier than June 1 and must be completed no later than Sept. 15.

The following conditions apply to all Take the Summer Off Program participants:

- During the period of summer leave, health insurance premiums must be paid by the employee, including that portion which is usually paid by the employer. Since this represents a substantial cost, employees are encouraged to think carefully about the financial impact of enrolling in the program before they apply.
- Arrangements for credit union or other direct payments from the employee's paycheck must be made directly by the employee.

- Performance evaluation periods and payments may be affected by the period of absence without pay.
- Employees may apply in September of the year prior to the summer in which they wish to participate in the Take the Summer Off Program. If approved by [date], a salaried exempt employee may arrange to have his/her salary for the year spread-out over the full year so that paychecks will be received during the period of leave without pay. For example, if an employee is approved before [date] for two full months of leave for the following summer, the employee may request that his/her salary for the 10 months during which he/she will be working be spread out over the full 12-month period.

Forms and any additional questions regarding this program should be directed to the HR department. All forms and applications must be submitted in a timely manner to maximize participation opportunities.

35 Work Sabbatical Policy

If an opportunity arises for an employee to work or undertake a special project outside of the company for a period of six months or less, the employee may request a work sabbatical. Applicants must have been employed full-time by the company for at least three years and must meet the following criteria:

- The employee's work performance is superior and on quota.
- The employer deems that there are acceptable resources and adequate coverage available during the employee's absence.
- The employee provides a detailed description and documentation of the work opportunity.
- The employee understands and accepts that this is a leave without pay.
- The employee has not taken an unpaid leave of absence in the prior two years.

If an employee has secured an outside work opportunity of longer duration, such as a university fellowship or book contract, the employee may request up to a 12-month leave of absence as long as he/she has been a full-time employee of the company for five years. The above criteria also apply.

In the case of a fellowship, the leave of absence shall cover the duration of the fellowship only, but may not exceed 12 months.

No more than one employee per calendar year may be granted a work sabbatical. (*To be filled in by company*) are not eligible for work sabbaticals.

If the manager and the employee agree to all of the above conditions, then the following items should be discussed and the Work Sabbatical Leave Form completed and signed:

- The employee can opt to continue his/her selected benefits for the agreed-upon time period if he/she pays the entire premium to the company. The company will make the payments to the various insurance carriers on the employee's behalf. If the employee elects to continue his/her benefits, the company will notify each carrier in writing of the employee's leave of absence.

- If electing to continue his or her benefits, the employee must submit a check representing the full monthly payment, made payable to (*to be filled in by company*), no later than the fifteenth of each month. Failure to submit payment will cause the employee's benefits to end immediately.

- Employees choosing to continue their benefits must understand that the benefit coverage is for doctors and services within the location where they live and work. If the work sabbatical takes them to another city/state, then the coverage does not include being treated in that new location and the rules of the employee's health plan apply.

- Employees who opt to discontinue their benefits must understand that, upon their return to work, they will be treated as new employees and any waiting period and/or exclusion of pre-existing conditions may apply.

- Once the time period for a work sabbatical is agreed upon in writing, it cannot be extended without a written request for extension and approval by management. If it is shortened, prior notice to the supervisor also is required. The total leave taken may not exceed one year.

- The employee and supervisor agree and understand that the position will remain open and available when the employee returns. Should the employee fail to return to work at the end of the agreed period of time, the position will be terminated.

NOTE: This leave is not intended to be an extension of Family and Medical Leave Act, short-term disability/long-term disability and/or any other current benefit provided by the company. This policy does not constitute a guarantee of continued employment. Rather, employment with the company is on an "at will" basis.

36 Work Sabbatical Leave Form

I have read and understand all of the parameters of this request for leave, as per the Additional Leave/Work Sabbatical section of the HR Policy manual. I certify that I understand that:

I agree to return to work by_____ (date). I understand that failure to do so will result in my termination as an employee of [Company Name].

Should I need to adjust this return date, I will contact my immediate supervisor, and such extension is at his/her discretion. Such request must be made in writing.

I understand that under no circumstances may this leave extend beyond the guidelines established in the Additional Leave/Work Sabbatical policy. I will provide my immediate supervisor with two weeks' notice in advance of my return date.

I am eligible to elect the continuation of specific benefits during my leave, but I am required to pay the full cost of the premium. I have checked the boxes below to indicate which coverage I wish to extend. These coverages, along with the specific costs based on current elections, are as follows:

❑ Health coverage $ _____
❑ Dental coverage $ _____
❑ Short-term disability $ _____

❑ Life/AD&D $_____
❑ No election of benefits coverage

Total benefits premium of $_____ is due to (*to be filled in by company*) on or before the fifteenth of each month.

I further understand that if I do not elect to continue this coverage or if I allow my coverage to lapse, upon my return I will be treated as a new employee regarding the benefits indicated above.

All company policies are applicable during this sabbatical. I am aware that these policies and programs may be amended at any time and, depending upon the particular circumstances of a given situation, the company's actions may vary from written policy. This policy should not be construed as a guarantee of continued employment. Rather, employment with the company is on an "at will" basis.

Employee's Name _____Date _____

Supervisor's Name _____Date _____

HR Manager's Name _____Date _____

37 Voluntary Reduction in Force (RIF) Separation Program

The program intent is to allow for voluntary reductions in force for employees of XYZ. This Voluntary Reduction in Force Separation Program facilitates an employee's transition to retirement or early separation at-will and provides access to state financial assistance for the pursuit of career opportunities, creates opportunities for XYZ restructuring and assists XYZ in meeting its fiscal responsibilities. Use of this program has the same objective as other downsizing initiatives, that is, to allow XYZ to minimize the impact of downsizing by allowing employees to volunteer to be separated in lieu of another employee who is slated to be separated by RIF procedures. Some employees, who can afford to leave XYZ but, for instance, whose seniority standing precludes separation, would like to be separated by RIF in order to be eligible for entitlements, such as unemployment compensation. This program sets forth the framework under which employees can volunteer to be separated in order to save other employees from RIF.

Applicability

All employees both, exempt and nonexempt, union and non-union, are given consideration for participation if they are in an area where the workload is being reduced. Generally, employees occupying critical or hard-to-fill positions, or with critical knowledge or skills, will not be allowed to participate except with the approval of the project manager. Employee participation in the Voluntary RIF Separation Program is not an entitlement and is subject to the discretion of XYZ.

Definitions

- *Reduction in Force* (RIF): A customer-directed contract reduction resulting in downsizing of workload requirements and loss of related positions.
- *Voluntary Reduction in Force*: A reduction in force in which employees in selected task areas are allowed to volunteer for layoff. The selected task areas will generally align with contract reductions.

Policy

At its discretion, XYZ will initiate a Voluntary RIF Separation Program. This program may become necessary because of a lack of work or funds, or whenever it is advisable in the interest of economy to reduce the number of regular and/or probationary employees. The program's first step is to seek the necessary staff reductions through voluntary methods. This program is designed to benefit both XYZ and employees. Based on the following principles, approval of Voluntary RIF Separation Requests will be at the sole discretion of XYZ:

- Avoidance of involuntary layoffs
- Reduction in number of employees affected by mandated RIFs

A voluntary RIF separation is a separation approved by XYZ on the grounds that it serves a principle purpose noted above. Approval of a voluntary RIF separation means an employee will not be automatically disqualified when applying for unemployment compensation, as is usually the case when an employee voluntarily leaves employment. Individual employees must still meet the eligibility requirements of the Unemployment Compensation Program in order to receive benefits. XYZ will provide fair and consistent treatment of all individuals involved in the process.

To be eligible for the Voluntary RIF Separation Program, an employee must, prior to leaving employment, have been offered an opportunity to participate, or made a special request for a voluntary RIF separation.

The project manager may approve a voluntary RIF separation under the conditions described below:

    a. voluntary separation can be effected only during formal RIF, that is, only in circumstances where official RIF notices will be issued;

b. voluntary separation eliminates the need to serve displacement notice to another current employee;

c. voluntary separation results in a vacancy to be filled by an employee, from within the facility, who has already received displacement notice (the displaced employee must be fully qualified to fill the vacated position); and

d. matches of separation volunteers with those affected by the formal RIF will be based on similarity of their positions. Any position affected by the RIF can be identified for placement of a RIF separation volunteer, if separation of the RIF volunteer would result in the cancellation of a RIF separation action, and the subsequent placement of a RIF-affected employee.

Placements, which result in a promotion, are to be approved by the project manager. Human Resources should determine the best match for placement, considering qualifications for placement in the volunteer's position, the ability of the RIF-affected employee to do the work of the similar position, and cost effectiveness.

When there are more volunteers than needed and all are equally good matches, XYZ will process voluntary RIF applicants in order of seniority using the Service Contract Act seniority date.

When there are fewer volunteers than needed and there are equally good matches for displacement, XYZ will select RIF-affected employees for displacement in accordance with SPI 1327 for non-union employees and in accordance with the collective bargaining agreement for represented employees.

Volunteering for RIF separation under this policy is strictly a voluntary action on the part of any employee to whom this option is offered. Such employee shall not be forced or coerced in any way to volunteer for RIF separation.

Procedures

a. XYZ may, in accordance with the principles of this policy, attempt to reduce the number of employees within a department or job classification in order to avoid involuntary layoffs, by seeking separation volunteers.

b. After a RIF-affected employee has received notice of separation, XYZ will post a bulletin outlining procedures to make application for a voluntary RIF separation.

c. Separation volunteers will be issued RIF separation notices effective on the RIF effective date of the original displaced employee. The notice shall advise them of their entitlements under RIF.

d. Volunteers must sign a statement that they realize the action is irrevocable once they have been issued a RIF separation notice. However, XYZ may cancel the action if necessary.

e. Separation volunteers will be treated as involuntary RIF separations, with all entitlements.

38 401(k) Plan: Hardship Withdrawal Request

Please read the information and instructions at the end of this document before completing this form.

Section I. Participant Information

Employee Name: _____

Social Security Number (SSN): _____

Date of Birth (mm/dd/yyyy): _____

Address: _____

City, State, ZIP Code: _____

Daytime Telephone Number: _____

Section II. Reason for Hardship Withdrawal

1. Expenses for (or necessary to obtain) medical care that would be deductible from the participant's federal income taxes under *Internal Revenue Code* (IRC) Section 213(d), determined without regard to whether the expenses exceed 7.5% of adjusted gross income. Attach medical bills or estimates.

2. Costs directly related to the purchase of a principal residence for the participant, excluding mortgage payments. Attach the purchase agreement.
3. Payment of tuition, related educational fees, and room and board expenses for up to the next 12 months of post-secondary education for the participant, the participant's spouse, children, or dependent. Attach the tuition statement. (See plan description for the definition of "dependent.")
4. Payments necessary to prevent the eviction of the participant from his or her principal residence or to prevent foreclosure on the mortgage on that residence. Attach the eviction or the intent to foreclose notice.
5. Payments for burial or funeral expenses for the participant's deceased parent, spouse, children, or dependents. Attach invoices. (See plan description for the definition of "dependent.")
6. Expenses for the repair of damage to the participant's principal residence that would qualify as a casualty deduction from the participant's federal income taxes under IRC Section 165, determined without regard to whether the loss exceeds 10 percent of adjusted gross income. Attach invoices.

Section III. Available Options

Can this hardship be completely **or** partially relieved through the following options?:

- Reimbursement or payment by insurance or other sources? Yes/No
- The reasonable liquidation of assets, provided the liquidation would not itself cause an immediate heavy financial need? Yes/No
- The cancellation of elective deferrals under the 401(k) Plan? Yes/No
- Loans, including loans available from my 401(k) account?
Attach loan denials from a commercial source. Yes/No

If you answered "Yes" to any of the four questions above, you are ineligible for a hardship withdrawal until the option(s) for which you have answered "Yes" have been exhausted or until you can provide documentation that your hardship cannot be completely relieved through the source(s) indicated above.

Section IV. Request for Withdrawal

Do not withhold federal taxes from my withdrawal. I will be liable for all federal taxes that may result from this withdrawal, including penalties, if applicable.

I hereby request a withdrawal of my contributions from the [Company Name] 401(k) Plan because of an immediate and heavy financial hardship; this withdrawal may include the dollar amount necessary to satisfy the anticipated taxes and penalties that are incurred as a result of the withdrawal. The dollar amount requested is limited to the amount documented to meet the immediate hardship. I request that $ (gross) be distributed from my account.

Section V. Participant Certification

I request a hardship withdrawal to be made in accordance with the Plan Document, Internal Revenue Code, and my election. I understand that the company has the authority to approve or reject this request. I understand that federal income tax of 10 percent will be deducted from the amount approved unless I otherwise specify. I hereby certify under penalty of perjury that this information is true and accurate to the best of my knowledge. I understand that if my request is approved, any 401(k) Plan payroll deductions will be immediately canceled for a period of six months.

Signature:_____

Date:_____

Information

Your decisions regarding a hardship withdrawal will have financial consequences as well as income tax implications. Therefore, you may wish to obtain the advice of a tax advisor before you request a hardship withdrawal.

To meet the criteria for a 401(k) hardship withdrawal, you must first exhaust all other options. Refer to Section III.

You are prohibited for six months from contributing to any employee retirement benefit plan. You will be responsible for all federal and state income tax and applicable penalties on the amount withdrawn. Federal taxes will be withheld at a rate of 10 percent unless you request otherwise by checking the box in Section IV. State taxes will not be withheld unless you request otherwise by completing the applicable withholding certificate form. If you are younger than age 59½ or if this withdrawal is for anything other than medical expenses, you may be liable for an additional 10 percent federal tax penalty and an additional state tax penalty, if applicable. A 1099-R will be issued by January 31 of the following year for reporting purposes.

Once all necessary documentation has been received, your request will be reviewed and a decision will be rendered within 14 days. You will be notified in writing of the final decision.

Instructions

Section I. Participant Information
Complete the information requested.

Section II. Reason for Hardship Withdrawal
Check all boxes that apply. Please submit copies of documents. The purchase agreement must be signed by the buyer and the seller and include a closing date.

Section III. Available Options
Check "Yes" or "No" in response to questions.

Section IV. Request for Withdrawal
Check the box(es) that are applicable to your request and fill in the gross amount you want to be distributed from your account.

Section V. Participant Certification
Read carefully, sign, and date the form.

Mail the original form (do not fax) to:
[Company Name]
[Address]
[City, State, Zip]

39 Layoff and Recall Policy

If the company must reduce employment because of adverse economic or other conditions, layoffs and recall from layoffs generally will be conducted in a manner that is consistent with company requirements and in accordance with the procedures described below.

1. In the event that a layoff is expected, the company will attempt to communicate information about an impending layoff as soon as possible. However, management reserves the right to alter the layoff procedure and withhold information about the layoff as permitted by law in order to protect the company's interests.

2. Layoffs that are expected to be temporary generally will be handled according to the provisions of this policy. Selections for layoffs that are known to be permanent will be made according to this policy and then handled according to company termination of employment and severance pay policies.

3. Evaluation of the foregoing criteria shall be within the sole discretion of the company. Employees will be selected for layoff based on the following criteria:

- Promotion potential and transferability of skills to other positions within the unit
- Demonstrated current and past performance
- The needs of the company and specific projects
- Length of service with the company

4. An employee's length of service is measured from the original date of employment with the company, as long as there has not been a break in service greater than 30 days. During a layoff, employees with breaks in service greater than 30 days, but less than one year per break, are credited only for their time actually worked, i.e., the break time does not get counted unless required by law. Employees with a break in service greater than one year receive credit for service only from their most recent date of hire with the company.

5. Employees selected for layoff will be given as much notice as is required by law or as much as is reasonable under the circumstances.

6. Employees who are laid off will be maintained on a recall list for six months or until management determines the layoff is permanent, whichever occurs first. Removal from the recall list terminates all job rights the employee may have. While on the recall list, employees should report to the HR department if they become unavailable for recall. Employees who do not keep a current home address on record with the HR department will lose their recall rights.

7. Employees will be recalled according to the needs of the company, their classification and their ability to perform the job. Notice of recall will be sent by registered mail, return receipt requested, to the current home address on record with the HR department. Unless an employee responds to the recall notice within seven days following receipt of the notice or its attempted delivery, the employee's name will be removed from the recall list and the employee will no longer have any job rights with the company.

8. Credit for seniority will continue to accumulate during any layoff of 30 days or less. Employees laid off for more than 30 days and subsequently recalled within one year from the date of layoff will be credited with the years of service accumulated at the time of layoff.

9. If the layoff is expected to exceed 30 days, vacation pay equal to the number of unused vacation days accrued will be paid at the time of layoff. Employees who are laid off will not accrue vacation or sick leave during the layoff.

40 Low-Need Time

In the event that scheduled staff exceeds staffing needs, a supervisor may need to temporarily reduce hours. These temporary reductions in hours (low-need time) will be utilized in blocks of one hour or more on the basis of seniority and will not result in the loss of benefits. Low-need time is non-paid time.

Procedures for Low-Need Time

- If the supervisor knows far enough in advance of the diminished need for staff, or the reduction involves a shift currently being worked, the supervisor will first request volunteers.
- If no volunteers are forthcoming or the situation does not lend itself to requesting volunteers, the supervisor will assign low-need time on the basis of seniority within the same job classification unless specific skills are needed. The least senior employee scheduled on a shift will be required to take low-need hours. If more low-need hours are necessary, the hours will be given to the next least senior person scheduled for that shift.
- Low-need time can also be utilized for shifts currently being worked when staffing needs decrease during the shift. Such low-need time will also be assigned on the basis of seniority.
- Prior to assignment of low-need time, the supervisor will explore the possibility of floating the employee to another unit or area for which the employee is oriented and qualified.
- Employees who are assigned low-need time prior to the commencement

of a shift will be given a minimum of two hours notice. If a minimum of two hours is not given the employee will be paid the difference between two hours and the notice actually given.

- Employees who have reported for a shift of work and are assigned low-need time will be paid a minimum of two hours or the time actually worked, whichever is greater.
- Low-need hours are to be specifically marked on an employee's time card so appropriate credit can be given for benefit purposes.
- Employees will be encouraged to use paid time off (PTO) for low-need hours.

41 Separation Agreement and Release of Claims*

This Separation Agreement and Release of Claims ("Agreement") is made by and between Jane Doe ("Ms. Doe"), an individual, and ABC Company, a [INSERT STATE] corporation ("ABC").

WHEREAS, ABC is undergoing a reduction in force and restructuring that will result in the elimination or consolidation of the functions of Ms. Doe's position;

WHEREAS, ABC desires to provide Ms. Doe with some separation benefits to assist her in the transition resulting from the elimination of her position with ABC; and

WHEREAS, Ms. Doe agrees, in exchange for such separation benefits, to waive and release any and all claims that she may have against ABC.

NOW THEREFORE, in consideration of the mutual promises and releases contained herein and for other good and valuable consideration, the sufficiency of which is hereby acknowledged, the parties agree as follows:

Salary and Benefits Continuation. Upon the execution of this Agreement, the parties agree as follows:

* This sample courtesy of the Law Firm of Ray & Isler, Vienna, Va.

Ms. Doe shall be laid off from employment with ABC effective_____ (hereinafter the "layoff date").

Up to and including the layoff date, Ms. Doe also shall continue to be enrolled in all of ABC's benefits plans in which she is enrolled at the time of the execution of this Agreement.

Within 30 days following the layoff date, ABC shall provide Ms. Doe with payment for vacation accrued up to and including _____ .

On or before the layoff date, ABC will provide Ms. Doe with a reference letter in the form appended hereto as Attachment A.

Following the layoff date, Ms. Doe shall be entitled to any and all other rights or benefits afforded to other terminated employees of ABC, including, without limitation, the right to elect to continue, at her cost, coverage under the ABC health plan, in accordance with the health care continuation coverage provisions of the Consolidated Omnibus Budget Reconciliation Act of 1985 ("COBRA").

Release: Ms. Doe, on behalf of herself, her descendants, ancestors, dependents, heirs, executors, administrators, assigns, and successors, and each of them, hereby covenants not to sue and fully releases, acquits, and discharges ABC, and its subsidiaries and affiliates, past, present, future and each of them, as well as its owners, trustees, directors, officers, agents, servants, employees, stockholders, representatives, assigns, and successors, and each of them (collectively referred to as "ABC Releasees") with respect to and from any and all claims, wages, demands, assistance, support, rights, liens, agreements, contracts, covenants, actions, suits, rights to appeal, entitlements and notices, causes of action, obligations, debts, costs, expenses, interests, attorneys' fees, contributions, damages, judgments, orders and liabilities of whatever kind or nature in law, equity or otherwise, whether known or unknown, suspected or unsuspected, and whether or not concealed or hidden, which she has at any time heretofore owned or held against said ABC Releasees, including, without limitation, those arising out of or in any way connected with her employment relationship with ABC or her layoff or any other transactions, occurrences, acts or omissions or any loss, damage or injury whatever, known or unknown, suspected or unsuspected, resulting from any of them, committed or omitted prior to the date of this Agreement, and including, without limitation, claims for breach of contract, libel, slander, wrongful discharge, intentional infliction of emotional harm, or other tort, or discrimination or harassment based upon any federal, state, or municipal statute or local ordinance relating to discrimination in employment.

Indemnity Regarding Assignment of Claims: Ms. Doe represents and warrants that she has not heretofore assigned or transferred, or purported to assign or transfer, to any person, entity, or individual whatsoever, any of the claims released as set forth in Paragraph 2 above. Ms. Doe agrees to indemnify and hold harmless the ABC Releasees (as defined in Paragraph 2 above) against any claim, demand, debt, obligation, liability, cost, expense, right of action or cause of action based on, arising out of, or in assignment.

Entire Agreement: This Agreement constitutes and contains the entire agreement and understanding concerning Ms. Doe's employment and layoff, and the other subject matters addressed herein between the parties, and supersedes and replaces all prior negotiations and all prior agreements proposed or otherwise, whether written or oral, concerning the subject matter hereof.

Governing Law: This Agreement shall be governed by and subject to the laws and exclusive jurisdiction of the courts of the state of [INSERT STATE]. In the event that she breaches any of the provisions of this Agreement, Ms. Doe agrees to pay ABC's reasonable costs of prosecuting such claims, including attorneys' fees and costs.

Severability: In the event that one or more of the provisions of this Agreement shall for any reason be held to be illegal or unenforceable, this Agreement shall be revised only to the extent necessary to make such provision(s) legal and enforceable.

The parties acknowledge that they have read the foregoing Agreement, understand its contents, and accept and agree to the provisions it contains and hereby execute it voluntarily and knowingly and with full understanding of its consequences.

PLEASE READ CAREFULLY. THIS AGREEMENT INCLUDES A RELEASE OF KNOWN AND UNKNOWN CLAIMS.

ABC Company, Inc.

By: _____

Name:_____

Jane A. Doe

Title: _____

42 Reduction in Force Selection and Severance Pay

A reduction in force (RIF) occurs when changing priorities, budgetary constraints, or other business conditions require [Company Name] to abolish positions. A RIF can also occur when a position changes so significantly that the employee is no longer able to perform the required duties.

Selection for RIF

A reduction in force decision requires an evaluation of the need for particular positions and the relative value of work performed by specific employees so that the company can continue to provide the highest level of service possible with a reduced workforce. Determining the retention or separation of an employee includes an evaluation of the relative skills, knowledge, and productivity of the employee in comparison to necessary services. Length of service and other factors are also considered but receive less weight in the determination. [Company Name] determines priority for reduction in force within the following guidelines:

- Temporary employees performing the same work must be terminated before any employee with a probationary or permanent appointment, provided that a probationary or regular employee can perform the temporary employee's tasks.
- Reduction in force of permanent employees is based on the following factors:
- Which positions are most vital to the department in the delivery of services.

- Relative skills, knowledge and productivity of employees.
- Length of service of employees.
- Consideration of equal employment factors to avoid adverse impact on [Company Name]'s affirmative action goals.

Severance Pay

Severance pay is available for an eligible employee as determined in accordance with [Company Name]'s RIF determination process.

Calculating Severance Pay

Payment is based on length of service, salary at separation and age at separation (see Table 1). Payment is made in the same number of months as the number of months of pay. Payment is discontinued once re-employment is obtained.

Table 1

Years of Service	Payment
Less than 1 year	2 weeks base salary
1 but less than 5 years	1 month base salary
5 but less than 10 years	2 months base salary
10 but less than 20 years	3 months base salary
20 or more years	4 months base salary

An employee qualifies for an age adjustment factor at 40 years of age. To compute the amount of the adjustment, 2.5 percent of the annual base salary at separation, is added for each full year of age over 39 years of age (see Table 2 for an example). The total age adjustment factor cannot exceed the total service payment.

Table 2
Example: Age 59 Salary—$24,000/year, 20 years of service

Factor	Computation	Amount of Severance Pay
Service	$2,000/month for 4 months	$8,000
Age Adjustment	$24,000 x .025 x (59-39) = $12,000 (Age adjustment factor cannot exceed the service factor so the age factor is limited to $8,000.)	$8,000
	Total	$16,000 Distributed over 4 months

Table 3 includes deductions that must be withheld from severance payments.

Table 3

Deduction	Amount
Federal Withholding	Based on your current withholding status on W-4
Garnishments, Support Orders, Levies	Based on directive provided
Negative Leave Balances	Based on leave balances

The following deductions will not be withheld from severance payments:

- State income withholding tax (if permitted by your state)
- Medical insurances including health, dental and vision
- 401(k) and deferred compensation
- 401(k) loan payments
- Life insurance

Direct Deposit Enrollment

Severance payments, as well as any leave payout due, will continue to be directly deposited into the bank account currently set up. To change to a different account, please contact the payroll office.

Other RIF Benefits

A. Unemployment Insurance

Employees separated due to reduction in force are eligible to collect unemployment insurance provided they meet the normal eligibility requirements. Contact the local unemployment office to file a claim for unemployment compensation.

B. Leave Balances

Vacation Leave—Vacation leave is paid for a maximum of 240 hours.

C. Sick Leave

If an employee returns to [Company Name] within five years from separation date, it will be reinstated.

43 Involuntary Termination Policy

[Name of Company/Organization] reserves the right under employment-at-will to terminate any employee at any time when it considers the termination to be in the best interests of the company. When feasible, employees will be given warning that they are in jeopardy of losing their jobs. Involuntary terminations may occur as a result of lack of work, corporate restructuring, or for unacceptable performance and personal conduct.

Reasons for an involuntary termination may include but are not restricted to:

- Misrepresentation on employment application
- Chronic absenteeism
- Misconduct
- Theft
- Insubordination
- Intentional, wrongful, and unlawful misconduct

Employees may appeal an involuntary termination using the company's normal grievance policy and procedure.

44 Sample Letter: Benefits Changes Due to Reduction in Hours

To: [Name of Employee]

From: Director of Human Resources

Date: [Date]

Subject: Benefits Change Due to Reduction in Hours

As we recently discussed, due to lack of work for the foreseeable future, we have to reduce your work schedule from full time (40 hours per week) to part time (20 hours per week) effective on [date]. The reduction in hours results in a change in employment status that affects your benefits as follows:

Health Insurance: Your health insurance will terminate on the first day of the month following the effective date of your change to part-time status. However, you may continue coverage under COBRA for 18 months by electing this coverage and submitting a monthly payment of $ _____ by the first of each month. Enclosed is a COBRA notice and election form for you to complete and submit.

Life and Accidental Death and Disability Insurance: Your life and accidental death and disability insurance will terminate on the first day of the month following the effective date of your change to part-time status. Our policy has a conversion provision, which permits you to apply for an individual policy. Enclosed you will find information on this conversion option.

Paid Leave (Vacation, Sick, Personal Days): You will continue to accrue paid leave but on a prorated basis. As you will be working 20 hours per week, your accrual rate for paid leave will be one-half of that for a full-time regular employee. The section of [Name of Company] policy manual pertaining to paid leave and accrual rates is enclosed.

Holiday Pay: The policy of [Name of Company] is to pay any employee who works less than 40 hours per week for four (4) hours on each holiday the company observes. This policy section is also enclosed.

We are very pleased that you have decided to stay with [Name of Company] while working reduced hours and hope that economic conditions will improve to the level that we can again offer you full-time employment.

If you have any questions, please call or stop in.

Enclosures

45 Sample Letter: Layoff or RIF—Lack of Work

Dear Employee:

As you have known for the last several months, [Company Name] has experienced financial difficulties due to lack of work in our industry. Last year we introduced new products to replace those made obsolete by technological advances. Unfortunately, this action has not resulted in increased sales and work.

After reviewing our options, we have concluded that we must eliminate approximately (number) positions. It is with deepest regret that I inform you that your position is one that will be eliminated.

Within the next week, a representative from Human Resources will call you to set up a meeting. During this meeting you will learn about your separation benefits that include the services of an outplacement firm to provide counseling and assistance in finding another job quickly.

Please accept our appreciation for your good work during your employment with [Company Name].
Sincerely,
[INSERT NAME]

46 Sample Letter: Reduction in Force—Declining Sales

Dear Employee:

For several years now, we have been experiencing declining sales due to increased global competition. We have explored many options to improve efficiency and reduce costs. These measures have succeeded to some extent. However, in order to reduce costs further and become more competitive, we find that we must reduce our workforce.

Starting (date), we have to eliminate (number) exempt/salaried and non-exempt/hourly positions. The reduction in force will be based on business necessity by job category and then by performance ratings within the job category. We will provide you details on which job categories are affected and will meet with individual employees whose positions will be eliminated by the end of this week.

We have always valued and continue to value the contributions of all our staff and deeply regret the need for this action.

Sincerely,
[INSERT NAME]

47 Sample Letter: Termination Because of Layoff, Downsizing, Etc.

(Enter Date)

Dear (Name):

As you have heard, XYZ Company is (about to merge with ABC Company; or experiencing financial difficulties, or other reason for this action). I am sorry to have to tell you that you are to be (laid off or discharged) at this time. According to our plan, your last day at XYZ will be (a time in the near future).

(optional) You have had a good number of productive years with our company, and we are most appreciative of the good work you've done during your time with XYZ. We are offering you a generous severance package, in addition to outplacement services to assist you in finding new employment. Would you stop by the Human Resources Department at your earliest convenience to discuss outplacement services? HR will also explain your severance package, your eligibility for continuation of health care benefits, options for your 401(k) plan, and they can answer any other questions you may have.

We wish you the best of luck in your future endeavors.

Best regards,

HR Manager or Employee's Supervisor

Conclusion:
After the Layoff: How Are You Feeling?

Adrienne Fox

Every HR professional has a story to tell about a layoff. Good ones, bad ones, and truly heartbreaking ones. Conducting layoffs has become just another part of HR professionals' jobs, although not the best part. Veterans say it never gets easy to stand in front of a group of employees or look someone in the eye and say, "We have to let you go."

In these dour economic times, you may have just said those words—or may need to in the near future. In June 2008, employers took 1,643 mass layoff actions, resulting in 165,697 separations, the highest total for the month of June since 2003, according to the U.S. Department of Labor's Bureau of Labor Statistics (BLS).

Newspapers and business publications read like a veritable roll call of layoffs—20,000 here, 1,000 there, 80 there. The news may read like cold numbers to those not directly affected by reductions in force. But for HR professionals, each number represents a colleague, a contributor, or a friend.

Remember, "this is part of your job, no matter how much you dislike it," says Laurence Miller, Ph.D., a psychologist and author of *From Difficult to Disturbed: Understanding and Managing Dysfunctional Employees.*[1] "It's just like a pilot who has to deal with a failed engine or a police officer who has to deal with a shooting incident. When you take on the job of HR, you have to prepare for the likelihood of this happening."

Shared Pain

It may be particularly disheartening today because finding a new job takes longer than in the past. The average duration of unemployment rose nearly two weeks to 17.5 weeks from June 2007 to June 2008, according to the BLS.

HR professionals say they have one constant in getting through the painful task of conducting layoffs: each other. Commiserating with HR colleagues and other senior managers serves as one of the best emotional releases, psychologists say.

HR professionals also remind themselves that, in most cases, the layoffs were beyond their control—perhaps resulting from a downturn in the economy, an external event that hit one industry particularly hard or a change in business strategy. They turn to factors they can control: taking good care of those walking out the door. It gives them solace knowing they did what they could to prepare and help each employee make the transition to a new job.

But even with preparation, the internal pep talks about how they couldn't have prevented the layoff, and the good treatment of employees with severance and training, the act still takes an emotional toll. Psychologists involved in helping companies through employee assistance programs (EAP) have seen HR professionals worn down by the process.

Miller puts the feeling in simple terms: "No matter what, someone is going to hate your guts."

To be sure, the person losing his way of life, career, and, sometimes, identity suffers the most when a layoff occurs. But after a layoff, you need to make sure you're OK too.

Feelings

Libby Sartain, SPHR, has experienced layoffs from all angles—being laid off, delivering the news, helping others deal with the aftermath, and making the difficult decision that layoffs are necessary.

Having been laid off herself helped and hurt when it came to conducting layoffs, says Sartain, who served as chief people officer at Yahoo and Southwest Airlines, and who is now retired. "It helped because I knew what they were going through and could be compassionate. But it hurt because I knew how painful it is. Even though this is a business decision, it feels personal to the person laid off."

David Schwartz, founder of D N Schwartz and Co. in New York, a retained executive search firm, spent most of his career at Goldman Sachs, serving as vice president of HR during 2000-2002, when the firm laid off 120 of its 600 investment bankers. Schwartz was involved in the process and helped deliver the news to individuals.

"I never got used to it," Schwartz says about delivering the news. "It's horrible. In the situation where the general business landscape is bad, it's unlikely that these people will find jobs. You know it's going to take a year or so no matter how helpful you try to be."

Patricia Mathews, a member of the Society for Human Resource Management's (SHRM) Employee Relations Special Expertise Panel, describes the stages her mind goes through before, during, and after a layoff. She has been involved in layoffs at Occidental Petroleum's subsidiary OxiChem in western New York during the early 1980s, at Anheuser-Busch in St. Louis from 1983-1995 and at Argosy Gaming Co. in Alton, Illinois, from 1996-1998.

"Initially, your total focus is professional and structured and intellectual. Your mind goes there so you don't have to think about it," says Mathews, now president of Workplace Solutions, an HR consulting firm in St. Louis. "Then you start to think about the humanity, and you make sure the severance is good and the services are there. You are still in business mode."

She takes a deep breath before continuing. "And then there's the day you have to deliver the news, and that's the day that the emotional stress comes in. Everyone's nervous—the employees and senior management—because you don't know what to expect."

But, for Mathews, the buildup to the layoff event proves less stressful than the day after, when your focus turns to your own emotions. "You know it's a part of your job, and you tell yourself that and that you've made it the least painful possible," she says. "But in the back of your mind, the reality is: There are people who no longer have jobs, and they have families. You get this guilt, and you second-guess what could have been done to avoid the layoff."

For Mathews, the period of emotional letdown has lasted as long as six months. That was the case with the mass layoff she conducted at OxiChem in the 1980s, where she had to cut 3,000 people—half of the workforce—most of whom had been with the company for twenty years.

Psychologists say if such emotions become excessive or persistent, it's time to seek professional help.

Be Prepared

Knowing what to expect from employees' reactions can help HR professionals deal with the heightened anxiety common with layoffs.

"Being prepared will help HR people with their own feelings of guilt," says Hap LeCrone, Ph.D., a psychologist in Waco, Texas, and executive director of the Lake Shore Center for Psychological Services, a facility that provides EAP services.

When LeCrone is contracted by a company to help employees with the emotional aftermath of a layoff, he often will meet with the HR staff beforehand to discuss their concerns. "They are often fearful that people will come unraveled when they tell them the news or will become physically or verbally abusive," he says. "The HR manager wants tools to help deal with that. We discuss the variables that could happen and how to deal with each."

LeCrone will often be on-site when the message is delivered to a group of people. He keeps an eye out for body language—a person whose jaw tightens up, or someone who verbalizes to the person next to him or who gets up and storms out. "I'm there during and after to deal with anyone who acts out," says LeCrone. "That takes the pressure off HR. I tell them how to spot those people who continue to cry and are having a terrible reaction and look despondent or start throwing up in the bathroom."

Relying on Others

After HR professionals announce the layoff to employees and move out of the "business mode" mentality, they must take a moment to decompress with colleagues.

LeCrone advises HR professionals and surviving managers to come together in private soon after the layoff announcement to commiserate and learn how others are coping. In that privacy, those who have been through it before can help less experienced HR managers or supervisors. "The older dogs can help the younger ones know what to expect or if a reaction is normal," says LeCrone. "Find out how others are dealing, whether it is working out, taking days off or using the EAP."

Throughout the process, keep an eye out for signs of stress on your colleagues. "Quite a few times, I saw the stress become too much for my staff," recalls Mathews. "I would tell them to go home early or take a few days off and to come talk to me if they need to. The younger staff, especially, are surprised that it affects them the way it does."

Paul Gibson, SPHR, GPHR, chief human resource officer at Mattamy Homes in Toronto, warns of the "Norm" syndrome, referring to the episode in the television sitcom "Cheers" where Norm was given the responsibility of firing others in his company because he was empathetic and a good listener. Similarly, Gibson noticed that his manager of organizational effectiveness and talent acquisition Teresa Senisi had become Norm. "She is so good at presenting the story, helping people understand and getting them past the grief that she has become the person who everyone wanted to deliver the news," he says. Senisi is typically a positive person, he adds, but "I started to see a change in her, and I had to offload some of that responsibility."

Miller advises checking in with people you trust for an objective look at your demeanor and asking if they see changes in your behavior and outlook. Mathews' husband serves in that role. "He will see the emotional stress on me before I do, and he will reassure me and support me, and that helps," she says.

Outplacement counselors, hired to help employees transition into new jobs, can also be a valuable, objective resource for HR professionals. OxiChem and Anheuser-Busch brought in outplacement companies whose staff helped the HR teams by reassuring them that they had done a good job, says Mathews. "They're used to coaching and counseling, and they've seen it all before."

Gibson, who has conducted layoffs for previous employers, puts the events in perspective for his staff. "I remind people that we aren't doing the worst thing ever. We're not killing baby seals. And we get a chance to demonstrate respect and dignity through our humane process."

More than the Ax

"Respect" and "dignity" come up often when talking to HR professionals about layoffs. Once the business decision is made, they want to make sure people have the necessary tools to land on their feet. Indeed, creating a compassionate process helps HR deal with the guilt and grief of a layoff.

HR professionals need "to feel they have more to offer than simply the ax," says LeCrone. "If the HR person knows the company is providing outplacement services and EAP, it alleviates some of the stress."

Taking control has helped Gibson. "Yes, this is a dark thing we have to do, but it is also an opportunity," he says. "You can conduct the layoff with dignity and compassion and have pride in the process you helped create to help employees find other positions."

Even having a say in seemingly minor details can help—like what day of the week you give the news. "Do layoffs on a Monday or Tuesday morning, not on a Friday," explains Mathews. "If you do it on a Friday, the [separated employee] has the whole weekend to stew and he can't begin to look for a job until Monday."

Schwartz agrees and adds, "We didn't march people out of the office. We gave everyone a week or so to sort things out. We gave them three or four months in an off-site office to do a job search."

Being as humane as possible helps HR professionals stay connected to departing workers. "I count as personal friends and business colleagues a number of people I let go, largely because the firm had a very civilized approach to layoffs," says Schwartz.

The Incomprehensible

Civilized was not the word Daisy Wong would describe for her employer's layoff process. She worked as a graphic designer for a clothing manufacturer near San Francisco from November 2007 to March 2008 when she was cut during the second of three rounds of layoffs.

"It would have been better to do it all at once rather than piecemeal," says Wong, who asked that her real last name not be used. "After the first one, you think, 'Oh, OK, they want to cut back.' But then there's another round and then another, and you think, 'Couldn't they have planned this better?'"

The process also differed from one round to the next. "In the first round, the people laid off had to leave that day," she says. "In my round, I had one week's notice and my severance was small because I was just hired. In the third round, no one got severance and they had to leave that day."

Wong doesn't understand why she was hired in November only to be laid off a few months later. She even remembers a new colleague who saw her supervisor laid off on the new employee's first day on the job. "It doesn't seem like there was much foresight or planning from HR," she says.

It's Your Job

The need for workforce planning, including a recovery strategy, represents the biggest lesson for HR professionals conducting layoffs: "The company has a business need or you wouldn't need a layoff," says Sartain. "So, you have to ask the questions about workplace planning. Sometimes, executives will suggest [cutting] ten percent of the workforce, but that might not be the best strategy. The tendency is to cut all your bottom performers, but sometimes that means you get rid of a job you really need."

Needing to fill positions you have just eliminated doesn't make the layoff seem well-planned and doesn't help with survivor morale. "A layoff challenges you to make sure that the decision you made is the right one because you don't want to do it and then have to bring people back," says Jerome Carter, senior vice president of human resources at International Paper in Memphis, Tennessee. "These decisions shouldn't be made if they're not sound business logic."

No matter how emotionally draining, a layoff may be necessary for the company—and its surviving employees—to thrive. Make sound business judgments, have a plan in place that treats laid-off employees with dignity, and prepare yourself for the emotional toll.

"HR people are so used to taking care of others, but you have to take care of yourself," says Mathews.

"HR [professionals] shouldn't be left out to dry," adds LeCrone. "They need support, too. They are closest to survivors. And HR and line managers need to recover quickly for the organization to recover from a layoff."

Additional Resources

SHRM Toolkits

Bankruptcy Toolkit

The contents of this toolkit offer a compilation of resources to help gain understanding of the elements of bankruptcy and offer guidance to successfully manage the process of bankruptcy. This toolkit also covers the antidiscrimination component of the federal bankruptcy law, which protects employees and applicants from discrimination based on having filed for bankruptcy. Available at http://www.shrm.org/hrtools/toolkits_published/CMS_007345.asp#TopOfPage.

Layoff Toolkit

Many employers experience financial difficulties that force them to terminate employees. Whether it's called a layoff, reduction in force or downsizing, these employment actions can result in legal challenges and a remaining workforce that is demoralized and unproductive. With knowledge of state and federal laws and best practices for conducting these types of terminations, difficulties may be avoided. This toolkit provides you with these resources. It will help you handle layoffs and similar terminations legally, effectively and with consideration for your departing and remaining employees, thus preparing your business for recovery. Available at http://www.shrm.org/hrtools/toolkits_published/CMS_007359.asp#TopOfPage.

Termination Toolkit

Terminations come in two forms—voluntary or involuntary. Voluntary terminations in most cases are easy to handle: an employee provides a resignation of their intention to leave the organization and leaves within a specified period of time. Sometimes voluntary terminations can be complicated. An employer may be forced to release the individual prior to the designated date. This can turn a voluntary termination into an involuntary termination. Available at http://www.shrm.org/hrtools/toolkits_published/CMS_010695.asp#TopOfPage.

Unemployment Toolkit

Unemployment benefits, established in 1935 as part of the Social Security Act, provide a temporary source of income to unemployed individuals. Unemployment benefits are administered by each state and are funded through employer's taxes. States set the requirements on who is eligible to receive benefits, how long an individual must wait to receive benefits and how much of a benefit is received. They also determine which circumstances disqualify an individual for benefits. When a former employee is disqualified for benefits, the employer is not charged. Available at http://www.shrm.org/hrtools/toolkits_published/CMS_014556.asp#TopOfPage.

Workforce Planning Toolkit

Workforce planning is the process an organization uses to analyze its workforce and determine steps it must take to prepare for future needs. The process involves forecasting the future composition of the workforce, conducting a gap analysis between the current and future staff, deciding how to close any gaps, and determining whether the needs will be met by recruiting, training, or outsourcing. This toolkit contains resources that will help HR practitioners in this important part of their organization's strategic planning. Available at http://www.shrm.org/hrtools/toolkits_published/CMS_011649.asp#TopOfPage.

SHRM Books

Thomas P. Bechet, *Strategic Staffing: A Comprehensive System for Effective Workforce Planning*, 2d ed. (SHRM/AMACOM, 2008).

Wendy Bliss, *The Essentials of Managing Change and Transition* (SHRM/Harvard Business School Press, 2005).

Wendy Bliss and Gene R. Thornton, *Employment Termination Source Book* (SHRM, 2006).

Ken Carrig and Patrick M. Wright, *Building Profit through Building People: Making Your Workforce the Strongest Link in the Value-Profit Chain* (SHRM, 2006).

Wayne Cascio and John Boudreau, *Investing in People: Financial Impact of Human Resource Initiatives* (SHRM/Pearson, 2008).

Amy DelPo and Lisa Guerin, *The Essential Guide to Federal Employment Laws* (SHRM/Nolo, 2006).

Roger Herod, *Expatriate Compensation: The Balance Sheet Approach* (SHRM, 2008).

Sharon K. Koss, *Solving the Compensation Puzzle: Putting Together a Compete Pay and Performance System* (SHRM, 2008).

R.J. Landry, *The Comprehensive, All-in-One HR Operating Guide* (SHRM, 2006).

Jack J. Phillips and Patricia Pulliam Phillips, *Proving the Value of HR: How and Why to Measure ROI* (SHRM, 2005).

Seyfarth Shaw, *Understanding the Federal Wage & Hour Laws: What Employers Must Know about the FLSA and its Overtime Regulations* (SHRM/Seyfarth Shaw, 2005).

William J. Rothwell, Robert K. Prescott, and Maria W. Taylor, *Human Resource Transformation: Demonstrating Strategic Leadership in the Face of Future Trends* (SHRM/Davies-Black, 2008).

Mary F. Scott and Scott B. Gildner, *Outsourcing Human Resources Function: How, Why, When, and When Not to Contract for HR Services*, 2d edition (SHRM, 2006).

Other Books

Judith M. Bardwick, *One Foot Out the Door: How to Combat the Psychological Recession That's Alienating Employees and Hurting American Business* (AMACOM, 2007).

Bernard Baumohl, *The Secrets of Economic Indicators: Hidden Clues to Future Economic Trends and Investment Opportunities* 2d ed. (Wharton, 2007).

Karen Berman, Joe Knight, and John Case, *Financial Intelligence: A Manager's Guide to Knowing What the Numbers Really Mean* (Harvard Business School Press, 2006).

*John W. Boudreau and Peter M. Ramstad, *Beyond HR: The New Science of Human Capital* (Harvard Business School Press, 2007).

*Hugh Bucknall and Zheng Wei, *Magic Numbers for Human Resource Management: Basic Measures to Achieve Better Results* (Wiley, 2005).

Peter Cappelli, *Talent on Demand: Managing Talent in an Age of Uncertainty* (Harvard Business School Press, 2008).

Roger D'Aprix, *The Credible Company: Communicating with a Skeptical Workforce* (Jossey-Bass, 2008).

*Dale Dauten, *(Great) Employees Only: How Gifted Bosses Hire and De-Hire Their Way to Success* (Wiley, 2006).

*Amy DelPo and Lisa Guerin, *The Manager's Legal Handbook*, 4th ed. (Nolo, 2005).

Niall Ferguson, *The Ascent of Money: A Financial History of the World* (Penguin Press, 2008).

Jon Gordon, *The No Complaining Rule: Positive Ways to Deal with Negativity at Work* (Wiley, 2008).

*Thomas M. Hanna, *The Employer's Legal Advisor* (AMACOM, 2006).

Craig Karmin, *Biography of the Dollar: How the Mighty Buck Conquered the World and Why It's Under Siege* (Crown, 2008).

Ian I. Mitroff, *Why Some Companies Emerge Stronger and Better from a Crisis: 7 Essential Lessons for Surviving Disaster* (AMACOM, 2005).

Kerry Patterson et al, *Influencer: The Power to Change Anything* (McGraw Hill, 2007).

*Steve Pogorzelski and Jesse Harriott, *Finding Keepers: The Monster Guide to Hiring and Holding the World's Best Employees* (McGraw-Hill, 2007).

*Brette McWhorter Sember and Terrence J. Sember, *The Essential Supervisor's Handbook* (Career Press, 2007).

Available through the SHRMStore.

About the Contributors

Elizabeth Agnvall is a Washington, D.C.-based freelance writer.

Mary Birk is an attorney with Baker Hostetler in Denver, Colorado.

Jennifer Taylor Arnold is a freelance writer and editor in Baltimore, Maryland.

Peter Cappelli is the George W. Taylor Professor of Management and Director of the Center for Human Resources at Wharton University. He is the author of *Talent on Demand: Managing Talent in an Age of Uncertainty* (Harvard Business School Press, 2008).

Adrienne Fox, a freelance writer in Alexandria, Virginia, is a contributing editor and former managing editor of *HR Magazine*.

Lin Grensing-Pophal, SPHR, is a Wisconsin- based business journalist with HR consulting experience. She is the author of *Human Resource Essentials: Your Guide to Starting and Running the HR Function* (SHRM, 2002).

Rebecca R. Hastings, SPHR, is manager of SHRM's Online Diversity Focus Area.

Stephen Miller is an online editor/manager for SHRM.

Theresa Minton-Eversole is manager of SHRM Online's Staffing Management Focus Area.

Donna M. Owens is a freelance writer based in Baltimore, Maryland.

Gina Rollins is a freelance writer in the Washington, D.C., area.

Anne St. Martin, SPHR, CEBS, is the manager of express operations in SHRM's HR Knowledge Center.

Marcia Scott is the medical Director at Prudential's Group Life and Disability Insurance. *This paper is provided by the Society for Human Resource Management in cooperation with the Academy of Organizational and Occupational Psychiatry. The paper is produced for information purposes only and is not intended as medical advice.*

John Sweeney, GPHR, SPHR, is an HR Knowledge Advisor in the SHRM HR Knowledge Center.

Steve Taylor is a freelance writer based in Arlington, Virginia.

Peter Weaver is a freelance writer in the Washington, D.C., area.

Susan J. Wells, a business journalist in the Washington, D.C., area and a contributing editor of *HR Magazine*, has more than 20 years of experience covering business news and workforce issues.

Nancy Hatch Woodward is a freelance writer based in Chattanooga, Tennessee, and a frequent contributor to *HR Magazine*.

Endnotes

Chapter 3

[1] Peter Cappelli, *Talent on Demand: Managing Talent in an Age of Uncertainty* (Boston, MA: Harvard Business School Press, 2008).

[2] Peter Navarro, *The Well-Timed Strategy: Managing the Business Cycle for Competitive Advantage* (Upper Saddle River, NJ: Wharton School Publishing, 2006).

Chapter 5

[1] Hay Group, "Hay Group Slowing Economy Study—April 2008," accessible at http://www.haygroup.com/us/Expertise/index.asp?id=12076.

[2] Bureau of Labor Statistics, U.S. Department of Labor, "The Employment Situation: June 2008," reissued July 10, 2008, accessible at http://www.bls.gov/news.release/empsit.nr0.htm.

[3] Ben S. Bernanke, "The economic outlook," testimony before the Joint Economic Committee, U.S. Congress, April 2, 2008, accessible at http://www.federalreserve.gov/newsevents/testimony/bernanke20080402a.htm.

Chapter 6

[1] See American Staffing Association, "Staffing Employment Edged Down in Early 2008," May 27, 2008, accessible at http://www.americanstaffing.net/statistics/newsreleases/May_27_08.cfm.

[2] Kathy Gurchiek, "LINE Report: Softer Labor Market in June," SHRM, 5/23/08, accessible at http://www.shrm.org/hrnews_published/archives/CMS_025652.asp#P-8_0. Updated LINE reports can be accessed at http://www.shrm.org/LINE.

Chapter 7

[1] For information about how to purchase the surveys, visit http://www.naceweb.org/info_public/salaries.htm.

[2] Experience, Inc., "Gen Y Job Seekers Say It's Time for a Job Description Makeover," 2/11/08, accessible at http://www.experience.com/corp/press_release?id=press_release_1202748368612&channel_id=about_us&page_id=media_coverage_news&tab=cn1.

[3] Experience Inc., "It's Time for a Job Description Makeover," (2008), accessible at http://www.experience.com/pdf/recruiter_jd_whitepaper.pdf.

Chapter 9

[1] Career Protection, "Annual Layoffs Forecast: 2008 Executive Survey Finds Severe Job Cuts to be Made This Year," accessible at http://www.careerprotection.com/press.html.

[2] LINE reports can be accessed at http://www.shrm.org/LINE/.

Chapter 11

[1] SHRM Weekly Survey, "Assistance Organizations Are Offering to Help Employees Deal With High Gas Prices in 2008," May 6, 2008, accessible at http://www.shrm.org/hrresources/surveys_published/bydate/QOTWbydatetoc.asp.

Chapter 13

[1] Weichert Relocation Resources Inc., "WRRI Survey Tracks Real Estate Market's Effect on Corporate Relocation," 6/10/2008, accessible at https://www.wrri.com/jsp/news_show_article.jsp?nid=4250.

Chapter 14

[1] See Right Management's Press Release, "Right Management's Research Uncovers New Trends in Outplacement Changing Client Needs Driving Innovation in the Industry," June 28, 2007, accessible at http://phx.corporate-ir.net/phoenix.zhtml?c=65255&p=irol-newsArticle&ID=1020213&highlight=.

Chapter 15

[1] See "FSU researcher: As gas prices climb, employee productivity plummets," May 5, 2008, accessible at http://www.eurekalert.org/pub_releases/2008-05/fsu-fra050508.php.

[2] Edward A. Charlesworth and Ronald G. Nathan, *Mind Over Money and Stress Management: A Comprehensive Guide to Wellness* (Houston, TX: Biobehavioral Press, 1982).

[3] The May 2007 SHRM Weekly Survey, "What is your organization doing to help employees deal with 2007 gas prices?" 5/24/07, and the May 2008 SHRM Weekly Survey, "Assistance Organizations Are Offering to Help Employees Deal with High Gas Prices in 2008," 5/6/08, are accessible at http://www.shrm.org/hrresources/surveys_published/bydate/QOTWbydatetoc.asp.

Chapter 16

[1] Howard S. Dvorkin, *Credit Hell: How To Dig Out Of Debt* (Hoboken, NJ: John Wiley and Sons, 2005).

Chapter 18

[1] Transamerica Center for Retirement Studies, Press Release, "Economy Casts Dark Shadow Over Retirement Confidence," February 28, 2008, accessible at http://www.transamericacenter.org.

[2] Duke University/CFO Magazine Global Business Outlook Survey, December 2007, accessible at http://www.cfosurvey.org.

[3] Employee Benefit Research Institute, "Retirement Confidence Survey—2007 Results," April 2007, accessible at http://www.ebri.org/surveys/rcs/2007.

[4] Colette Thayer, "Preparation for Retirement: The Haves and Have-Nots," Research Report, AARP Knowledge Management, November 2007, accessible at http://www.aarp.org/research/financial/retirementsaving/retirement_prep.html.

[5] From a SHRM interview with Professor Keller on March 4, 2008.

Conclusion

[1] Laurence Miller, *From Difficult to Disturbed: Understanding and Managing Dysfunctional Employees* (New York: AMACOM, 2007).

Index

401(k), 34, 62, 66, 68, 69, 74-77, 79,
130-132, 144, 154

A

absenteeism, 34, 62-64, 103, 111, 146
acquisition, 11, 40, 56
adverse treatment, 84
affirmative action goals, 143
Age Discrimination in Employment Act
    (ADEA), 85, 92
alternative work schedules, 110, 111
appraisals, 39
at-will, 81, 122, 125, 146
audit, 51
    technology audit, 51

B

baby boomers, 58
bankruptcy, 34, 35
    personal bankruptcy, 75
benchmarks, 13
benefits, 16, 46
    employee benefits, 25
    employee retirement benefit plan, 132
    health care benefits, 154
    loss of benefits, 136
    retirement/pension benefits, 25
    separation benefits, 138
    transportation benefit
        transportation benefit plan (TBP), 96
        transportation benefits account, 99
    unemployment benefits, 1, 80-1
Bernanke, Ben S., 24
Budget metric, 16
Bureau of Labor Statistics, 1, 156
burnout, 102
business

business conditions, 9
business cycles, 1
business downturn, 91
business forecast, 24
business literacy, 21
business necessity, 152
business plan, 17, 39
business strategy, 2
business updates, 21
internal business processes, 8
buyer value option (BVO), 54, 55

C

candidate advocate, 60
career counselors, 59
career transition services, 60
certified bargaining unit, 94
COBRA, 139, 148
collective bargaining agreement, 84, 128
college students, 31
communication, internal, 17
compensation, 9, 27
    market compensation practices, 24
    total compensation cost, 21
    unemployment compensation, 126, 127
compensatory time credits, 95
compensatory time off, 94
competencies, 3, 4, 39
    organizational competencies, 3
compressed work schedules, 104
compressed work week(s), 46, 102-104
compressed workers, 103, 105
confidence, 75
Congress, 24
contingency planning, 15
contingent labor, 49
contingent workers, 85
contingent workforce, 49

contract reductions, 127
contract workers, 26
contractors, 9
cost(s)
    cost-cutting, 17
    human capital costs, 16
    labor costs, 18, 49
    payroll costs, 80
    reduced costs, 22
    temporary-worker costs, 16
cost of living raise, 46
counseling
    consumer credit counseling services, 35
    credit counseling, 69
    debt counseling services, 62
credit woes, 74

D

demographics, 39
Department of Labor, 57
disability, 122
disciplinary actions, 44
discrimination, 44
discriminatory charges, 84
disparate treatment, 84
displaced workers, 1, 56, 57, 60
displacement notice/notification, 60, 128
distress, 12, 13
downsize/downsizing, 10-13, 16, 56, 84, 126

E

economic
    cycle(s), 14, 24, 40
    downturn, 2, 38, 52, 78, 157
    expansion, 18
    problems, 48
    recovery, 18
    security, 76
    slump, 40
    turbulence, 8, 15
    uncertainty, 14, 24
employee
    behavior, 11
    benefit(s), 25, 72
    contract employees, 49
    efficiency, 50
    employee-directed retirement plans, 75
    forgivable loan, 72, 73
    handbook, 81
    resistance, 11
    retention, 18
    retirement benefit plan, 132
    RIF-affected employee, 129
employee assistance program (EAP), 35, 36,
    61, 62, 64, 157, 159, 160
employees
    displaced employees, 19
    exempt employees, 80, 114
    non-union employees, 128
    nonexempt employees, 114
    problem employees, 12

temporary employees, 9
unstable employees, 35
employer
    employer's matching contribution, 75
    loyalty, 44
    match, 78
employment applications, 81
entrepreneurial spirit, 42
Equal Employment Opportunity Commission
    (EEOC), 84
expenses
    consulting expenses, 16
    operating expenses, 2
    transportation expenses, 96, 98

F

fair employment practice laws, 84
Fair Labor Standards Act (FLSA), 80, 94, 05
Family and Medical Leave Act, 122
financial
    assistance, 62
    awareness, 35
    challenges, 34, 67
    concerns, 74
    consequences, 132
    counselors, 67
    difficulties, 154
    education, 62, 68, 69, 78
    health, 67
    literary programs, 67
    plan, 77
    planning decisions, 79
    problems, 34, 35, 36
    stress, 34, 62-65
    woes, 64
flexible schedules, 46
flexible work, 108, 109, 114
flextime, 105, 110, 114, 116
foreclosures, 8
furlough, 4, 80

G

Generations X and Y, 58
Great Depression, 2
gross domestic product, 24
gross national product, 24
group distress, 11

H

health care, 25, 66
    health care benefits, 154
health insurance premiums, 118
hiring freezes, 40
hiring slowdown, 49
holiday pay policy, 110
home values, 74
human capital, 3
human resources (HR), 1, 3, 4, 8-10, 12, 14-
    18, 22, 28, 29, 38, 39, 48-54, 59, 60, 69,
    70, 76, 128, 135, 156-162

I

income
adjusted gross income, 131
income tax implications, 132
insurance
unemployment insurance, 144
investment education, 76

J

job
category, 152
definitions, 13
descriptions, 31, 32
functions, 58
qualifications, 31
satisfaction, 13, 67
share/sharing, 111-113
uncertainties, 74

L

labor
contingent labor, 49
costs, 18, 49
needs, 14
pool, 18
layoff(s), 1-4, 8, 17, 18, 20, 25, 38, 39, 41,
42, 44, 56, 80, 81, 84, 85, 90, 91, 127,
134, 135, 138, 139, 140, 156-162
involuntary layoffs, 127, 128
layoff date, 138, 139
layoff process, 161
recall from layoffs, 134
leadership failure, 13
leave
additional leave, 124
leave allocation practices, 103
unpaid leave of absence, 120
vacation leave, 144
line managers, 15, 42, 162
low-need time, 136, 137
loyalty, 17

M

mandatory vacations, 18
market slowdown, 54
merger(s), 11, 40, 56
mid-career workers, 58
morale, 3, 20, 41, 44, 46, 102

N

non-disparagement agreement, 81
non-disparagement clause, 82

O

off-boarding, 51
onboarding, 50, 51
on-site wellness program, 62
operating efficiency, 2, 22
organizational culture, 17

organizational dysfunction, 11
organizational effectiveness, 159
outplacement, 56-59, 150
candidates, 58
counselors, 160
services, 154
outsourcing, 40
overtime, 9, 94, 95, 103, 110, 114

P

paid time off (PTO), 137
payroll deductions, 96, 132
performance, 1, 134
appraisal systems, 39
criteria, 44
documentation, 44
evaluation periods, 119
goals, 81
issues, 44, 64
management system, 39
poor performance, 12
problems, 44, 64
ratings, 152
reviews, 44
product elimination, 42
productivity, 13, 70, 102
anticipated productivity growth, 14
increased productivity, 67
productivity capacity, 18
reduced productivity, 34, 62

R

recession(s), 1,2,15, 17-19, 24, 25, 40, 42,
74, 79
recovery strategy, 161
recruiters, 27, 30
recruiting, 28, 29, 49
recruitment, 8, 18, 28, 30
reduction in force (RIF), 44, 51, 80, 81, 91,
126-128, 138, 142, 144, 152
RIF determination process, 143
RIF separation, 126, 127, 129
RIF-affected employee, 128, 129
voluntary reduction in force, 126, 127
reduction in hours, 136, 148
redundancy/redundancies, 40
relocation
managers, 54
options, 27
policies and practices, 54
program costs, 55
reorganization, 90, 91
restructuring, 49, 56, 138
restructuring programs, 2
retention, 16, 42, 49, 67
bonuses, 42
efforts, 18
staff retention, 110
retirees, 16
retirement, 77
employee retirement benefit plan, 132

employee-directed retirement plans, 75
employer-sponsored retirement plans, 76
nest eggs, 75
planning, 67, 79
plans, 66, 74, 75, 77
return on investment (ROI), 29, 50, 52
revenue enhancement, 22
rightsizing, 40

S

sabbatical, 18, 120, 121, 124, 125
salary/salaries, 18, 25
secession planning, 49
senior management, 8, 9, 76, 158
seniority, 85, 91, 136
separation agreement, 81, 82, 138
separation benefits, 138
severance, 59, 157, 158, 161
   package(s), 27, 154
   pay, 134, 143
      plan, 91
   payments, 44, 144
shutdowns, 20
sick leave, 63
soft economy, 21
staffing, 9, 14, 25, 28, 29
stock market, 79
stock prices, 74
strategy, 14, 16
stress, 34-36, 62-65, 102, 158, 159
summer off program, 118, 119

T

talent, 9, 16, 27, 42, 60
   acquisition, 160
   management activities, 28
   management applications, 49
   management system, 49
   management vendor, 52
tardiness, 34
technology, 48-53
telecommuting, 9, 46, 100
termination, 81, 146
   involuntary termination, 1, 82, 146
transitioning workers, 60
turnover, 13, 41, 44

U

unemployment, 157
   unemployment benefit programs, 1
union(s), 1, 103, 126
unpaid time off, 80

V

value creation activities, 22
vendor management solution, 49
virtual work arrangements, 27

W

wage assignments, 64
wage garnishment, 67
Worker Adjustment and Retraining
   Notification (WARN) Act, 90
workforce
   contingent workforce, 49
   future workforce, 14
   needs, 15
   planning, 14, 39, 49, 161
   practices, 9
   reductions, 59, 84
   workforce experts, 15
workload projects, 14
workplace demographics, 58
wrongful discharge, 44